The Rothschilds at Waddesdon Manor

EX LIBRIS

GILBERT S. KAHN

The Rothschilds

at Waddesdon Manor

Mrs. James de Rothschild

THE VENDOME PRESS
New York. Paris. Lausanne.
Distributed by The Viking Press

Acknowledgements for permission to
reproduce photographs are made to
the following:
The Illustrated London News for
illustrations of Queen Victoria's visit
to Waddesdon
The National Trust
The Countryside Commission
(photograph of the Store Room at
Waddesdon).
William Wood (photograph of the
aviary)

First published in 1979 by William Collins Sons & Company Ltd.
All rights reserved
Distributed in 1979 in the United States of America by
The Viking Press, 625 Madison Avenue, New York, N.Y. 10022

Library of Congress Catalog Card Number: 79-51261
ISBN 0-670-60854-8
Printed in Great Britain

TO THE NATIONAL TRUST

Introduction

WHEN MY HUSBAND DIED in 1957 and bequeathed Waddesdon Manor to the National Trust, their first care was to enable the public to visit the house as agreeably as possible. Their second priority was the longer-term objective of producing a complete catalogue of the contents of the house.

During the 21 years since the catalogue was first mooted, ten volumes have been published out of an anticipated total of seventeen. Yet although the complete series will one day give all the known provenance of the works of art in the bequest, the story of the house itself and of those who lived in it will still be missing.

I am trying to fill this gap because, by good fortune, I have probably learnt rather more than most about the people who created Waddesdon, who lived in it and transformed it, stage by stage, into what it has now become.

For 56 years I have been closely associated with many of its inhabitants and thanks to the date of my birth and marriage I became a member of the Rothschild family at a time when many of an older generation were still alive. They could clearly remember events which now seem infinitely long ago and were kind enough to share their memories with me and pander to my eagerness to learn all that they could tell me. In this way I was given the opportunity of understanding at least a few of the factors which impelled some of the family to reach decisions which have had a great impact on my own life. But my main source of information was my husband whose interest in his family was intense and whose knowledge of it was unrivalled.

The story of Waddesdon Manor divides itself naturally into its four different periods of ownership. They are those of three Rothschilds, Baron Ferdinand, his sister Alice and their great-nephew James; and finally, the National Trust in whose possession Waddesdon will, I hope, as in a fairy-tale, live happily ever after.

D. de R.

Baron Ferdinand de Rothschild 1874-1898

THE FIRST ROTHSCHILD to be known as an inhabitant of Frankfort lived there in the mid sixteenth century; the first to be known as a collector of works of art was Mayer Amschel (1744–1812), the founder of the banking firm whose influence on international finance derived from his appointment as financial adviser to the Elector of Hesse in 1801. It was Mayer Amschel's collection of rare coins and his skill as a chess player which first aroused the interest of the Elector, who later placed all his financial concerns in his hands. Mayer Amschel had five sons; the eldest remained in Frankfort, but the other four were sent to open banking houses in what were then, financially, the four most important countries of Europe—Austria, England, France and the Kingdom of the Two Sicilies. The five brothers were closely knit as a family and they operated their banks as a single unit, but with the passage of time these banks have lessened in number. The first to go was the Naples branch which was closed in 1869 after the Bourbons had had to leave the city; the next was Frankfort which ceased to exist in 1901, when Baron Willy, the Rothschild in charge of it, died leaving only two daughters. From that date the remaining banks became independent entities. Finally, the Vienna branch closed when Hitler invaded Austria. Now, only the London and Paris houses remain.

The five sons of Mayer Amschel all married; only his eldest son, Amschel, had no children. In the course of time the progeny of the other four sons intermarried continuously—in some cases for three succeeding generations. Such intensive inbreeding seems to have sustained a natural aptitude for finance as well as a distinct scientific bent. Common to all was a flair for quality and a love of collecting, whether it was of works of art, books or butterflies.

I knew intimately the youngest son of Mayer Amschel's youngest son; he was my father-in-law, Edmond. I also knew quite well the widow of Salomon, one of his elder brothers. Edmond himself married Adelaide, the grand-daughter of his father's brother Mayer Carl of the Naples branch; her range of family knowledge was singularly complete. Most people have eight great-grandfathers: my husband, thanks to intermarriage, had only one—Mayer Amschel. Whenever I am asked what

Baron Ferdinand de
Rothschild

9

relation he was to any other Rothschild it always seems simpler to say he was a cousin. This answer has the merit of truth but in most cases it would be possible to say that he was also an uncle or a nephew or a great-nephew. This multiple relationship sometimes played havoc with the mode of address used by members of the family, in the old days, outside England. My father-in-law told me that since his earliest youth he had been accustomed to '*tu-toyer*' his well-liked cousin Mathilde; on his marriage to her daughter he found it not only embarrassing but quite difficult to remember to conform to the rigid convention of the day and refer to Mathilde, thereafter, as '*Ma chère Belle Mere*' and employ the more formal '*vous*' whenever he spoke to her.

Baron Ferdinand de Rothschild, who was alone responsible for the existence of Waddesdon Manor and its surrounding estate, was a great-grandson of Mayer Amschel. Born in Paris in 1839, he was a younger son of Baron Anselm who had married Charlotte, a daughter of N. M. Rothschild of London. Shortly after his birth his father was sent, first to Frankfort and then to take charge of the family bank in Vienna. Baron Ferdinand's childhood in Frankfort and Austria was uneventful, interrupted only by a hugely enjoyed expedition to visit the 1851 Great Exhibition in London. His relations with his father were always distant: they never understood each other. However, his adoration for his mother was unlimited. To quote his own words: 'Children, like dogs, feel instinctively who it is who genuinely loves them. All my love went to my mother, who indeed sacrificed the whole of her short life to the care and tuition of her young family. I could hardly bear to be out of her sight; my happiest moments were when I was recovering from an illness and she nursed me and stayed at my bedside, telling me stories of which I never tired. My mother was my guardian angel, the one being around whom my existence revolved'.

Both his father and his mother contributed to his early awareness and love of works of art, which became the over-riding interest of his life. Writing of his childhood he said: 'In the early forties we resided in Frankfort, spending the winters in the town and the summer at a villa close by. As soon as the swallows made their appearance my father's curiosities were packed and stored away in a strong-room, where they remained until the cold drove us back again from the country. It was my privilege on these occasions to place some of the smaller articles in their old leather cases, and then again in the winter to assist in unpacking them and rearranging

* Baron Ferdinand de Rothschild's unpublished *Reminiscences* written in 1897.

10

Baroness Anselm de
Rothschild (1807–1859),
mother of Baron Ferdinand,
after a portrait by Sir
Thomas Lawrence

them in their places. Merely to touch them sent a thrill of
delight through my small frame. Long before I was born my
father had acquired a collection of Dutch pictures from Holland.
Day after day I would reverently study them, learning under
my mother's tuition to distinguish a Teniers from an Ostade
or a Wouvermans from a Both . . . But my happiness was
greatest when Professor Oppenheim was announced. He was a
painter of no special merit but he was a friend of the family,
and all we children had to sit to him for our portraits—which
in days not far distant will probably adorn the steward's or
the housekeeper's room. I readily forgave him the severe
trials of patience to which he subjected me, because he was

11

one of my father's chief purveyors of works of art. In those days there were no curiosity dealers in Frankfort worthy of the name, but his work took Professor Oppenheim into many private houses, where he occasionally discovered and picked up a fine old German cup, which he then brought to my father. I cannot describe the joy I felt when he unpacked some quaint Nuremberg or Augsburg tankard, or the figure of a man, a lion or a stag, which was weighed and bought by the weight. Oh! for those good old days when the artistic merit of a cup was of no account to its possessor, and he merely valued it according to the number of ounces it contained.'

The first tragedy of Baron Ferdinand's life came when his mother died in 1859; he was then nineteen years old. He was deeply attached to his two brothers and four sisters, but after his mother's death he felt he had no future in his father's austere house. England beckoned him as being in some way a link with this mother; within a few months he journeyed to London and then decided to stay there. His father, Baron Anselm, made no effort to force his son to take an active part in the family firm; he appears to have contemplated this son's interest in the arts and his lack of interest in banking with toleration. Baron Ferdinand, however, viewed his father's somewhat sporadic activity as an art collector with less equanamity. 'My Father might have formed a matchless collection' he wrote 'as he lived in a country where for years old works of art were deemed worthless. But his taste was limited to a small range as he cared for minute articles only, besides his time was too much occupied with business to devote much of it to other pursuits. When I left Vienna for London in 1860, I had many opportunities of offering him works of art, but he rarely availed himself of them. Many and many a time dealers showed me some fine article for which I had not space in my humble lodgings or which I had not the means to acquire and which I then offered to my Father—but as a rule he declined them'. Despite Baron Ferdinand's feelings of frustration, some thirty works of art which are now at Waddesdon come from Baron Anselm's collection; the majority are indeed snuff-boxes, miniatures or other 'minute articles'— not very helpful when the time came to furnish large empty rooms.

Baron Ferdinand's decision to settle in London proved to be a happy one; he fell in love with his first cousin Evelina, the daughter of Baron Lionel de Rothschild of the English branch, and his mother's niece. He became a British subject at the joint wishes of both himself and his prospective parents-in-law and, in July 1865, he and Evelina were married, with

3-inch high gold flask in the shape of a shell. c. 1740

Egg in gold, agate and enamel inscribed 'Rien d'agreable Eloignez de Vous'. The mis-spelling of 'éloigné' makes it probable that it was made in England, rather than France, c. 1760

Disraeli making a particularly felicitous and flowery speech at the wedding. They bought a house in Piccadilly and for eighteen months Baron Ferdinand learnt what perfect bliss could be, but it was not to last. His wife was injured in a railway accident and, as a result, died while giving birth to a still-born son. The inscription he placed on her grave, inspired by the Psalms and the Proverbs, may give the key to his feelings:

'If I ascend up into heaven, thou art there
If I lie down in the grave, behold I find thee.
Even there, thy hand leads me and thy right hand
supports me.
She opened her life with wisdom and in her speech
was the law of kindness.
My darling wife'.

Once again he was forlorn and lonely and the fact that he had glimpsed paradise only enhanced this feeling.

He had evidently planned with his wife to play a useful part in life from the background of a beautiful home, but although his sister Alice, then a girl of nineteen, decided to devote her life to his to relieve his loneliness, for some eight years he was numbed by sorrow. Doubtless he was advised that new sights and sounds might take his mind off his misery. He travelled to Russia alone and spent some time there in evident despondency. Even when pressed to take his pick of many wonderful works of art belonging to a Princess Galitzine which were shortly afterwards to be put up for sale, he was unable to rouse himself from his sorrow. In his *Reminiscences* he records: 'On entering the Princess's Palace and seeing the many fine pictures, the furniture, the sixteenth century works of art, I lost my breath. No amateur ever had such an opportunity, and possibly will never have the like again . . . I alas was still very inexperienced, moreover I was bewildered and hustled, and finally being in deep mourning I was not in the mood to take advantage of the opportunity'. All he bought was a topaz cup as a present for his father-in-law and 'a very inferior picture of the School of Snyders' for himself. Within a short time the majority of Princess Galitzine's possessions had found their way through dealers to the Wallace Collection.

On his return home he busied himself in planning and building the Evelina Hospital for Children in Southwark as a memorial to his wife. The hospital, which he purposely placed in one of the most crowded and poorest parts of London, had beds for a hundred children. It was formally opened by the Lord Mayor of London in 1869 who, in his speech,

A group of gold boxes
Top row left to right:
Gold Piqué snuff box with
miniature after Nattier, 1760
Gold & enamel travelling
inkpot, c. 1750
Bonbonnière in gold, enamel
& mother of pearl with
miniatures of the Bombelles
Family.

Bottom row left to right:
Swiss snuff box in gold &
diamonds, late 18th century
Gold enamel needlecase,
c. 1765
Double snuff box in gold &
agate, mid 18th century.

stressed that it was the first establishment for the cure of the sick which he had seen where emphasis had been put on the provision of light, air and space. Possibly through the building and the maintenance of the Evelina Hospital Baron Ferdinand became interested in the support of other hospitals. He was a generous donor, particularly to the Hospital for Consumptives in the Brompton Road, and St. George's Hospital at Hyde Park Corner, which was within a stone's throw of his own house in Piccadilly.

His sister Alice, having decided to live permanently in England, began by renting a house on Wimbledon Common, but joined her brother during the winter months at Leighton House, Leighton Buzzard, from where they hunted with the Whaddon Chase and the Tring Staghounds. Before long, the house next door to Baron Ferdinand's in Piccadilly became available and Miss Alice (as she was always known) seized the opportunity to become his near neighbour in London. Indeed they pierced a communicating door between the two houses, thus establishing the future pattern of their lives, separate but together.

At his death Baron Ferdinand left all his correspondence to his sister, it is thought with instructions that she should destroy it. Apart from the scarce family anecdotes of the period it is therefore only through reports issued by various charities,

Page from Baron Ferdinand's
Livre d'Or

Aerial view of Waddesdon

through memoirs and diaries of the time, and from snippets from the newspapers that it is possible to find any clue as to the sort of life Baron Ferdinand led during the eight years following his wife's death. It is obvious that he was active in various charitable fields and that he was making an increasingly wide circle of friends in London. Some of them were leading figures in the literary and artistic world. In 1873, he started keeping a *Livre d'Or*—an album in which he asked his friends to write or draw something. Among the first to do so were Anthony Trollope, Robert Browning and Sir John Millais. He was also making political friends; Gladstone and, of course, Disraeli added their contributions in 1873, as did John Lothrop Motley, then American Minister in London, who was famous as the author of the *Rise of the Dutch Republic*.*

It was while hunting that Baron Ferdinand first saw the magnificent views which can be glimpsed from the top of the hill on which Waddesdon Manor now stands, and, when his father died in 1874, he found himself provided with the funds

* The present Lord Rothschild reproduced Baron Ferdinand's *Livre d'Or* as his Roxburghe Club book (Cambridge University Press, 1957).

17

to build a house there and realise the plans he had first formulated with his wife.

The best and most detailed account of the building of Waddesdon Manor was written by Baron Ferdinand himself only about a year before he died. He said he wrote this because of the many enquiries he had received from his friends who wanted to know how he had managed to tackle such a vast enterprise in such a comparatively short time. If I were asked for my own views on *why* he did so I think, in racing parlance, I would say it was out of Loneliness by Artistic Craving. I can, however, think of no better way of describing the building of Waddesdon than by quoting from Baron Ferdinand's own account. This is what he wrote:

'In the autumn of 1874 I purchased from the Duke of Marlborough, by private treaty, his estate of Waddesdon and Winchendon, which had been put up for sale at Tokenhouse Yard in the spring of the year but withdrawn as the reserve price had not been reached. It then consisted of 2,700 acres to which I have since added about 500 acres. I had been looking out for a residential estate for some time, and could I have obtained one I should not have acquired this property, which was all farm land, chiefly arable, with neither a house nor a park, and though comparatively near London, was at a distance of six miles from Aylesbury, the nearest railway station. But there was none other to be had; there was not even the prospect of one coming into the market, and I was loath to wait on chance. So I took Waddesdon with its defects and its drawbacks—of which more hereafter—perhaps a little too rashly. I was buoyed up with the illusions and beguiled by the belief that within four years it would be connected with Baker Street by a direct line of railway, the first sod of which had not yet been turned. This much could be said in its favour; it had a bracing and salubrious air, pleasant scenery, excellent hunting, and was untainted by factories and villadom.

As soon as the contract was signed I set out for Paris in quest of an architect, and decided on the late M. Destailleur, whose father and grandfather had been architects of the Duke of Orleans, while he himself had risen to fame by his intelligent and successful restoration of the Château de Mouchy. M. Destailleur accompanied me back to England to choose the site for the house. This being settled, he left me fully supplied with instructions, while Monsieur Lainé, a French landscape gardener, was bidden to make designs for the terraces, the principal roads and plantations. It may be asked what induced me to employ foreign instead of native talent of which there was no lack at hand? My reply is, that having been greatly impressed by the ancient Châteaux of the Valois during a tour I once made in Touraine, I determined to build my house in the same style, and considered it safer to get the design made by a French architect who was familiar with the work, than by an English one whose knowledge and experience of the architecture of that period could be less thoroughly trusted. The French sixteenth century style, on which I had long set my heart, was particularly suitable to the surroundings of the site I had selected, and more uncommon than the Tudor, Jacobean or Adam of which the country affords so many and such unique specimens. Besides, I may mention that M. Lainé was called in only after Mr Thomas, the then most eminent English landscape gardener, had declined to lay out the grounds for reasons he did not deign to divulge.

By the side of the grand *châteux* of the Touraine, Waddesdon would appear a pigmy. The castle of Chambord, for example, contains 450 rooms, the smallest of which would dwarf the largest at Waddesdon. But its main features are borrowed from them; its towers from Maintenon, the château of the duc de Noailles, and its external staircases from Blois, though the latter, which are unglazed and open to the weather, are much more ornate. Though far from being the realisation of a dream in stone and mortar like Chenonceaux, M. Destailleur's work had fairly fulfilled my expectations.

M. Destailleur was a man of the highest capacity in his profession. He was a purist in style, painstaking, conscientious, and of the most scrupulous honesty. During the eighteen years of my relations with him there was never the smallest difference between us. But he was dilatory and unpractical. He had not the faintest conception of the needs of a large establishment, sacrificed the most urgent household requirements to external architectural features, and had the most supreme contempt for ventilation, light, air and all internal conveniences. This, perhaps, need not have surprised me, for he and his numerous family lived huddled together in a small and musty house in a dingy back street which I never entered without a shudder. It took me many an hour to convince him that ladies need space for their gowns and their toilette, and men want rooms in which they can move at their ease and perform their ablutions. The delay in the first start, however, was only partly his fault. He submitted a plan to me at the end of a year on a scale of such grandeur that I begged him to reduce it, and another long year was spent on the preparation of a second and more modest proposal. This I sanctioned, though it did not quite satisfy me. 'You will regret your decision' he said to me at the time; *'one always builds too small'*. And he prophesied truly. After I had lived in the house for a while I was compelled to add first one wing and then another; and a greater outlay was eventually incurred than had the original plan been carried out, not to speak of the discomfort and inconvenience caused by the presence of the workmen in the house. Though more picturesque the building is less effective, and while spreading over so much ground it is less compact and commodious.

As soon as the architect, the landscape gardener and the engineers had settled their plans, we set to work, but at the outset were brought face to face with a most serious consideration. This was the question of the water supply, as the few springs in the fields were not to be relied on in a drought. The Chiltern Hills fortunately contain an inexhaustible quantity of excellent water, which an Aylesbury company works with much skill to the advantage of the immediate neighbourhood and profit to its shareholders. Not a moment was lost in coming to terms with the Company, laying down seven miles of pipes from the county town to the village and thence to the projected site of the house, and building a large storage tank in the grounds. This subsequently proved insufficient for our wants, as one dry summer the supply failed, and but for the Manager's energy, who sat up all night at the Works sending us up water, we should have been compelled to leave the next day. To obviate the recurrence of a similar difficulty another and larger tank was constructed.

Then we had some trouble with the foundations of the house. We planned to build it on the crown of Lodge Hill, as it is called; small, but steep with its highest point being 64 feet above sea-level, it commands a panoramic view over several counties. The part of the hill we had selected as the site of the house consists of sand, and the foundations having been proceeded with for some months proved not to have been set deep enough, as they suddenly gave way. The whole of the brickwork had then to be removed and thirty feet of sand excavated until a firm bottom of clay was reached. I now began to realise the

Opposite Destailleur's elevation of the North front

The North front as it was built

Overleaf Preparing the site. Landscaping the Park. Laying the foundations of the house

20

importance of the task I had undertaken. But the difficulty of building a house is insignificant compared with the labour of transforming a bare wilderness into a park, and I was so disheartened at first by the delay and the worry that during four years I rarely went near the place. Slowest and most irksome of all was the progress of the roads, on which the available labourers of the neighbourhood were engaged supplemented by a gang of navvies under the direction of Mr Alexander, a London engineer, and M. Lainé. The steepness of the hill necessitated an endless amount of digging and levelling to give an easy gradient to the roads and a natural appearance to the banks and slopes. Landslips constantly occurred. Cutting into the hill interfered with the natural drainage, and despite the elaborate precautions we had taken, the water often forced its way out of some unexpected place after a spell of wet weather, tearing down great masses of earth. Like Sisyphus, we had repeatedly to take up the same task, though fortunately with more permanent results. The stone for the house which came from Bath, and most of the bricks which came from all parts of the country were conveyed

Stonemasons working at
Waddesdon, c. 1876

24

Chimneys at Waddesdon

on a temporary steam tram from the railway direct to the foot of the hill, up which the trucks were drawn on rails by a cable engine. Other materials for the building, as well as for the farmsteads, cottages and lodges, and the trees and the shrubs, had to be carted some miles by road. Percheron mares were imported from Normandy for this purpose, and they proved most serviceable, for though less enduring they travelled faster over the rough ground and were much cheaper than Shire horses.

The Percherons were employed principally in connection with the cartage of large trees which were brought from all parts of the neighbourhood, and for the moving of which into the highways the telegraph wires had to be temporarily displaced. They were transplanted with huge balls of earth round their roots, and were lowered into the ground by a system of chains, having been conveyed to the required spot on specially constructed carts, each drawn by a team of sixteen horses. The trees answered their purpose for a time, for they quickly clothed and adorned the bare hill. But if I may venture to proffer a word of advice to anyone who may feel inclined to follow my example—it is to abstain from transplanting old trees, limes and chestnuts perhaps excepted, and even these should not be more than thirty or forty years old. Older trees, however great may be the experience and skill of

25

The South front seen from the foot of the hill

Opposite Exterior of the Morning Room

the men engaged in the process, rarely recover from the injury to their roots, or bear the change from the soil and the climatic conditions in which they have been grown. Young trees try your patience at first, but they soon catch up with the old ones, and make better timber and foliage.

In 1880 I first slept in the so-called bachelors' wing, and in 1883 in the main part of the house. We had a grand housewarming in the month of July of that year, though the stables were not yet built, and the horses and carriages we required had to be accommodated in tents and in the village inns. The stables were built the following year from plans made by my stud groom, my builder, Mr Condor—than whom I have never met a more trustworthy businessman—and myself. Only the elevations were designed by M. Destailleur, and no other architect was ever called in for the alterations and additions subsequently carried out at Waddesdon. The whole credit of the work is his. I must take my full share of whatever blame there be. 'You should always begin with your second house', a lady once wittily said to me. But could this paradox be put into practice the second house would be as much open to criticism as the first. However great

26

your experience may be, you cannot arrive at perfection. I was anxious from the outset to sacrifice every consideration to ensure comfort, and for this reason determined against the introduction of a central hall, which, in my opinion, is fatal to all comfort; or, if made into a cosy and liveable apartment, condemns every other sitting-room to complete solitude. But a hall is, nevertheless, an indispensable feature in a country house of any size, and the want of a large room where my friends could all meet and read and write without disturbing each other was so much felt, that in 1889 I built one of this kind, which though not in a central position has to some extent at least redeemed the error I had made.

A word may be expected from me concerning the internal decoration of the house. In this M. Destailleur took but very small part. I purchased carved oak panelling in Paris for several of the rooms to which it was adapted by various French and English decorators. Most of this panelling came from historic houses; that in the Billiard Room from a château of the Montmorencis; that in the Breakfast Room and the Boudoir from the hôtel of the Maréchal de Richelieu in the street which was named after his uncle the great Cardinal and which has now been transformed into shops and apartments; the Grey Drawing Room came from the convent of the Sacré Coeur, formerly the hotel of the duc de Lauzun, who perished on the guillotine; and the Tower Room from a villa which was for some time the residence of the famous Fermier-Général Beaujon, to whom the Elysée also belonged.

The ornamental ceilings are either replicas of those of the rooms from which the panelling was taken, or copied from ones still in existence in Paris. The old mantel-pieces I secured from houses for which they were made; the one in the East Gallery was in a post-office, formerly the residence of the celebrated banker, Samuel Bernard. The modern mantel-pieces are copied from old models.

My grateful thanks are due to those who from first to last assisted me in my undertaking. They, too, may have remembered me kindly. M. Destailleur was entrusted by the Empress Eugénie with the construction of her house and church at Farnborough, and M. Lainé by the King of the Belgians with important works on his estates. These commissions they owed—the former indirectly, the latter directly—to me. Of M. Lainé I have nothing to say but praise. Still, I may be pardoned for mentioning that he only designed the chief outlines of the park; the pleasure

The breakfast room. The panelling came from the duc de Richelieu's house in Paris, demolished in the nineteenth century.

28

grounds and gardens were laid out by my bailiff and gardener according to my notions and under my superintendence; while all the farm buildings, model cottages, and lodges were built by a local architect, Mr Taylor of Bierton.

Waddesdon now has its hotel, its village hall and reading-room, its temperance and benefit societies, and its inhabitants are prosperous and contented. The Metropolitan, now called the Great Central Railway, sets down passengers at a station not a mile from the park gates, and my visitors are spared the tedious drive from Aylesbury, on which I expended many an epithet during twenty-two long years. A few more plantations are required to furnish the park, otherwise, save a judicious 'Keep', there is little the hand of man can still do. Time must be relied on to improve the house by colouring the masonry and giving it that rich mellowness of tone which age alone can produce, and beautify the grounds by allowing the trees to grow and expand. A future generation may reap the chief benefit of a work which to me has been a labour of love, though I fear Waddesdon will share the fate of most properties whose owners have no descendants, and fall into decay. May the day yet be distant when weeds will spread over the garden, the terraces crumble into dust, the pictures and cabinets cross the Channel or the Atlantic, and the melancholy cry of the night-jar sound from the deserted towers.'

Waddesdon proved to be the ideal focus Baron Ferdinand needed for the expression of his undoubted talents—not only artistic, but organisational, and incidentally gave him limitless opportunity for his love of ameliorating the life of others in a practical way. His wish to share at least some of the good things of life with his immediate neighbours became apparent as soon as the work at Waddesdon was started. The *Bucks Herald* reported with some amazement that when piping the Chiltern Hills' water to Waddesdon for his own use he should have arranged for the village also to be provided with 'the first pure and clean water it had ever had'. Equal surprise seems to have been evoked by the repeated celebrations Baron Ferdinand organised to mark the completion of each stage of the building of his house. Detailed reports exist of the dinners he gave—followed by fireworks—to all those who had taken part in the building work and the creation of the park. The first of these festivities, to celebrate the placing of the cornerstone, was held in a marquee from which this essential bit of masonry could be admired. 'The well loaded tables presented

Cottages at the entrance to the stable drive before they were rebuilt by Baron Ferdinand

The Village Hall at Waddesdon, built by Baron Ferdinand

31

a nice appearance before they were attacked' we are told, and 'a very substantial repast was served hot'. One wonders how this culinary miracle was achieved, for some hundreds of people, on a bare hill-top, nearly a mile from the village.

These celebrations were only equalled in size and apparent jollity by the annual 'School Treats' the Baron now instituted for the children of the surrounding villages and their parents. Within a few years these were so heavily attended that the *Bucks Herald*, while stressing the pleasure given by the tea, games, military bands and prizes provided on these festive occasions, warned that when they took place all roads to Waddesdon were so choked with horse traffic as to be a danger to the *bona fide* traveller.

Evidently, Baron Ferdinand very quickly learnt the truth of his architect's warning 'One always builds too small'. As the house was first designed, both he and his sister each had a bedroom and sitting-room on the first floor, and this would have left only five bedrooms free for guests in the main building and three more in the bachelors' wing. Even allowing for marital bed occupancy, this must have soon seemed in-adequate for the size of house-party which was fashionable in the hey-day of the Marlborough House period of entertainment.

There was almost certainly another reason for the continual 'improvements' Baron Ferdinand made to his house; this was his craving for works of art which, in their turn, called for space. Many were bought direct from other private owners or from such trusted dealers as Agnew, Colnaghi and Wertheimer, but in the eighties and nineties of the last century oppor-tunities for acquisition from all sorts of sources were endless, and indeed Baron Ferdinand was besieged with offers which he found irresistible and which often inconvenienced his finances. Being a sleeping partner in the family bank, he was dependent on its senior partners' decisions as to when the distribution of any profits should be made, and I remember my father-in-law's description of Baron Ferdinand impatiently panting to receive the wherewithal in order to be able to acquire some particularly longed-for work of art.

He had begun collecting when he was a very young man. His first major purchase was a Sèvres *Vaisseau-à-Mat*, one of the magnificent *pot-pourri* vases in the shape of a sailing ship which were so difficult to fire that only eleven were ever made by the royal factory. This acquisition, which is now one of the glories of the Grey Drawing-room, was quite beyond Baron Ferdinand's financial resources at the time. He records: 'I was unable to pay ready money for this piece of china— the best I possess—and blush to confess that I discharged my

Sèvres *vaisseau-à-mat*. Only eleven of these 'ships' are known to exist, of which three are at Waddesdon.

32

debt by instalments extending over two years. During these two years, I hid the 'ship' in a cabinet afraid to own it lest I should be scolded for my extravagance by my Uncles, of whom I stood in considerable awe'. It was not until his father's death in 1874 that he inherited the means to build Waddesdon or buy most of the works of art with which he furnished it including, eventually, two more Sèvres *Vaisseaux-à-Mat*.

In choosing pictures and furniture for Waddesdon Baron Ferdinand was guided not only by a sure feeling for quality but also by his sense of history and a particular knowledge of France in the eighteenth century. Through his purchase of objects made by the superb Parisian craftsmen of that time he was able to bring to life, to a remarkable extent, one of the most civilised phases of European history. He was successful in mingling French pictures and furniture with eighteenth century English portraits, for which he had a special liking.

Today, the propinquity of Gainsborough's 'Pink Boy', for instance, and the writing table made by Benneman for Louis XVI seems particularly happy, as does the same artist's portrait of Lady Sheffield in the neighbourhood of a Savonnerie carpet and Riesener *commodes*. But the Baron did not confine himself to English and French pictures; he also loved and bought the works of Dutch masters and the paintings of Guardi. Often it was not only beauty but historical association which appealed to him. I am sure that he derived much pleasure in acquiring such things as the writing table presented to Beaumarchais by his friends in 1781, or the essay on the rivers of France written by Louis XV, when he was a child, which was then printed and bound under the boy's own eyes, so that he should understand the intricacies of book production.

Baron Ferdinand had very definite ideas about the decoration of the rooms in which his purchases were to be placed. In his 'Reminiscences' he wrote: 'From the fall of the old regime in France until the beginning of the Second Empire the style of the decoration of French houses of the seventeenth and eighteenth centuries was condemned or ignored. In England, the early Italian, the Queen Anne or no style, had long been preferred; pictures, cabinets and china of all periods being usually placed against a damask or plain background. It was lavish or simple, often its merits were great, but the decoration was never 'French'. In France the style of decoration remained French, but it was a bastard nineteenth century style, graceless and tasteless, borrowing hardly a single feature from its predecessors. Whether it is to the credit of my family or not may be a matter of opinion, but the fact

The Green Boudoir. This is one of the three rooms at Waddesdon whose panelling came from the 18th century house in Paris of the Maréchal duc de Richelieu.

The South front seen across
the garden

remains that they first revived the decoration of the eighteenth
century in its purity, reconstructing their rooms out of old
material, reproducing them as they had been during the reigns
of the Louis'.

Baron Ferdinand was particularly fortunate in building
Waddesdon just at the time when much of the 'old material'
to which he refers was available for purchase. In the 1860's
Baron Haussman, the Prefect of the Seine, had almost completed
his work of driving great new streets through the heart of
Paris. In making these wide boulevards many old houses had
been knocked down and the superbly carved eighteenth
century panelling with which some of them had been decorated
was on the market. The beauty of the furniture and pictures
at Waddesdon seems to me to be immeasurably enhanced by
being seen against this background which Baron Ferdinand
imported from France.

His overwhelming interest in the manner of life and
decorative ideas of past centuries also led him to collect such
things as eighteenth century book plates and trade cards as
well as illustrated books of that period, many of which give
instruction in such minor arts as ironwork, penmanship, hair-
dressing and horsemanship. They indeed bear witness to the
extraordinary scope of his historical interest. The older he got,
the earlier became the period by which he was attracted. One

34

Some of the gardeners

of the dealers from whom he bought told me that it was only in the last years of his life that he turned his attention to the collection of the Renaissance objects which are now in the British Museum.

In his career as a collector he did not, of course, have the field to himself. Quite apart from several members of his own family in England, Germany, France and Austria, who were eager to acquire works of art of all kinds, there were many

The stable staff, c. 1900

Miniature of a lady, c. 1640 in contemporary gold and enamel frame. English

Gold and tortoiseshell bonbonnière with miniature by Peter Adolf Hall

formidable rivals, when he was a young man, such as Lord Hertford. Later, in England, he found many competitors in the auction rooms, like Lord Dudley or Mr. Mills (later Lord Hillingdon).

But many things were not bought at auction. There was an accepted routine in the Art Dealers' world which, I believe, was practised with notable success. As soon as some particularly desirable object had fallen into a dealer's hands, it was his habit to call on one of his more notable clients at a convenient moment, and start a conversation, I gather, on these lines: 'I have brought this to show *you*, Baron, as I would like *you* to have it. I know XYZ would buy it immediately, but I wanted you to see it first, as I think it would look so well in your house. But please treat this confidentially, as I would not like it to be known that I have given you first refusal'. If such a goad to rivalry did not happen to be successful the dealer would then pass on to the next most likely buyer, with just the same story, suitably adjusted.

On some occasions Baron Ferdinand did not buy alone but combined with other members of his family to make and share some major purchase. My father-in-law and Baron Ferdinand were two of a consortium of cousins who bought the outstanding Van Loon collection which included the lovely paintings by Metsu and Willem van de Velde which are now at Waddesdon; and Baron Ferdinand and his cousin Mayer jointly instructed the dealer Alexander Barker to buy from the hôtel de Villars in Paris the carved mirror surrounds by Nicolas Pineau which were numerous enough to provide the decoration of the dining rooms at both Waddesdon and Mentmore.

As soon as Waddesdon was in any way habitable and furnished, Baron Ferdinand started asking his friends to stay. A careful study of his visitors' book reveals the growing size of his house-parties, and it was not long before he began to build again, adding more bedrooms for guests and others for their personal attendants. Increased facilities had also to be provided for the production of food. Incredible though it may seem today, not only was a Still Room added to the kitchen— for the production of breakfast rolls, home-made jam, tea, coffee and soft drinks—but a further kitchen had to be provided for the use of a pastry cook who specialised in puddings, ices and sweetmeats. In yet another kitchen, a baker made bread only. The preservation of food had also to be considered before the days of frigidaires and deep freezers. In the middle of a plantation on an eminence just off the Stable Drive, which still goes by the name of 'Ice House Hill', ice was preserved on the shelves of a stone hut put up on this completely shaded site. In place of the high windows of the northern wall of the kitchen—now the public tea-room—there was a cluster of larders. The largest had its walls pierced with tiny holes, sufficient to aerate, but small enough to debar flies; partitioned down the middle, one side was kept for meat, and the other for fish. The larders themselves were concealed by a high grassy bank, planted with tall trees and flowering shrubs. Finally, a laundry was installed behind the stables. This included ample living accommodation for five laundry maids who were expert in wielding antediluvian irons and mangles—doubtless the most up-to-date of their kind at the time—to produce an endless supply of pristine sheets with frilled edges which, for the feminine guests, were adorned with lace and ribbons. The drying ground of the laundry was marvellously conceived, concealed from all prying eyes by a huge hedge surrounding the grass lawn on which long lines of cord, stretched from end to end, sustained the washing swaying gently in the sheltered breeze.

Roll-top desk made by Riesener in 1774 for Madame Adelaide, daughter of Louis XV

The dining room: the Beauvais tapestry was designed by Boucher: the carpet is late 18th century Aubusson

Baron Ferdinand was a perfectionist which is a costly attribute, but nevertheless, there are many instances at Waddesdon of his ingenious economies. For instance, all the vast windows have secure inner shutters made of wood. In the day-time, these are folded back and only the last panel of any shutter is visible, and this is made of beautiful oak. All the other panels are made of the plainest deal, since, by night, when the shutters are closed, they are completely concealed by the curtains drawn in front of them. Again, in all the rooms, the floors are of rough planks; only in the few rooms where the carpets do not extend from wall to wall is there a border of exquisite parquet.

In appearance Baron Ferdinand was a slight, spare, bearded man of medium height. Oddly enough, we know his weight which was only 10 stone 6 lbs when fully dressed in shooting clothes. This information is entered in the book at Sandringham in which the weight of all visitors there was recorded in King Edward VII's time. In spite of recurring bouts of illness which irked him from childhood until his early death, the Baron

Detail of one of the mirrors in the dining room at Mentmore which came from the same room in the Hôtel de Villars in Paris as the mirrors in the dining room at Waddesdon

was by no means physically inactive. He rode well although he could not walk far and certainly not uphill without the aid of a friendly push. During his 59 years he attempted much and achieved a great deal, quite apart from the visible evidence of Waddesdon.

He was Liberal Member of Parliament for Aylesbury from 1885 until he died, 14 years later. He was also an active member of the Bucks County Council; a Trustee of the British Museum and a keen Mason (hence the Ferdinand de Rothschild Lodge). He worked hard at these and numberless other part-time responsibilities. He also travelled widely, both in Europe and further afield in his yacht, the *Rona*. The diary he kept of a journey he made to South Africa in 1896 shows remarkable prescience; the conclusions he reached about the probable consequences of the treatment of the black population at the end of the last century have been proved unhappily true, some eighty years later. Yet, despite all this activity, he was an omnivorous reader; his large library of historical memoirs and diaries is a most treasured part of his successors' inheritance.

As Liberal member for Aylesbury, Baron Ferdinand did not often speak in the House of Commons, but the subjects which moved him to do so are, perhaps, indicative of his character. When the extension of the Marylebone railway line to a new goods terminal, near Lord's Cricket Ground, was hotly opposed, for the reason—among others—that smuts and dirt might sully the gowns of ladies attending the Oxford and Cambridge, or Eton and Harrow matches, Baron Ferdinand would have none of it. He made a forthright speech outlining the benefits a goods line would bring to the smallholders of Buckinghamshire who wished to sell their produce in the Metropolis. On another occasion, when there was a row about the British Ambassador in Paris being ordered not to attend the opening of the Great Paris Exhibition, because it was thought this occasion was a disguised celebration of the centenary of the French Revolution, Baron Ferdinand provided a detailed historical count-down of events which did much to clarify his fellow members' somewhat hazy notions of French history. But his most persistent political endeavour was to bring about some improvement in the pay and working conditions of the Post Office Telegraph Clerks. These men, before the introduction of the telephone, formed the vital link in any form of quick communication both within the British Isles and abroad. The Government acknowledged that all the clerks had to be qualified in some 'electrical understanding', and to be fluent in French and German, but were, apparently, quite content that they should be paid a maximum of £120 a year; that they should be required to work an average of 14 hours a day, including Sundays; that they should be given no time for meal-breaks and were, in fact, liable to punishment if they were found trying to nibble any form of food during their working hours. For five long years, Baron Ferdinand persecuted a particularly obdurate Postmaster General with questions about the Telegraph Clerks' pay and conditions. Invariably the reply was that 'the exigencies of the service' determined the hours of work, and that the Clerks' pay, their minimal chances of promotion and their occasional need to eat, were all 'under consideration'. Tiring eventually of the Government's stone-walling attitude, Baron Ferdinand, with the help of Lord Compton, managed to bring in a Private Member's Bill, in which, in effect, the Government was accused of maltreating its own servants. Baron Ferdinand believing, perhaps rightly, that Lord Compton's powers of eloquence were greater than his own, was content to second Lord Compton's masterly exposition of the Telegraph Clerks' miseries, stressing, in his own speech, the callousness of a Government which had made it seem advisable to adopt the most unusual course of promoting a Private Member's Bill to regulate the treatment of public servants. Like all his previous attempts, this one was not immediately successful; the Bill was defeated. But within a year the Government did see fit to raise the Clerks' pay by £10 a year, and to reduce their daily hours of work. Feeling perhaps, however, that he had been culpably overgenerous, the same Postmaster General with whom Baron Ferdinand had battled for so many years, decided at the same time to dock the authorised annual holidays of the Telegraph Clerks by one week. That, however, was this particular Postmaster General's swan song. The Government was thrown out, and it was a new Postmaster General who had to face Baron Ferdinand's continuing questions about why the award of an extra £10 a year made the Telegraph Clerks' need for an adequate holiday any the less.

In May, 1886, when the Liberals were once more in power, Mr Gladstone brought in his proposals for Home Rule for Ireland, to which many members of his own party were hotly opposed. Led by Lord Hartington—a frequent visitor to Waddesdon—the dissident Liberals formed the Liberal-Unionist party, and voting with the Tories, threw out Mr Gladstone's Home Rule Bill. From the names to be found in the visitors' book at Waddesdon it can, perhaps, be assumed that some of the discussions which preceded this horrendous split in the Liberal party must have taken place there; certainly, Baron Ferdinand took a prominent part in the birth of the new party.

For anyone who fondly believes in the inevitable progress
of the human race, any comparison of the political questions
of the Baron's day with those of our own, can only be dis-
quieting. Separated by a distance of ninety years, the Hansards
of the 1880s and the 1970s display a similar agonised anxiety
about what to do about Ireland. In 1886 Baron Ferdinand took
part in a debate on the reform or abolition of the House of Lords,
and debates on the Fishing Industry, the optimum size of the
Army and the possibility of the Government providing employment for the unemployed are common to both eras. Even a
Select Committee on Gaming was set up while Baron Ferdinand
was a Member of Parliament which, one feels, may well have
considered questions dealt with by the Royal Commission on
Gambling which has been sitting under the Chairmanship of
Baron Ferdinand's relative, Lord Rothschild. Despite two
world wars and the loss of an Empire, at Westminster it seems
that *plus ça change, plus c'est la même chose.*

Although Baron Ferdinand's personal contributions to the
great debates in the House of Commons were infrequent, it is
probable that Waddesdon was often a centre for political
debate outside the House. All the political lions stayed with
him frequently; the signatures of Gladstone, Rosebery, Joseph
Chamberlain and Balfour appear again and again in the

Two of Baron Ferdinand's
parliamentary supporters

visitors' book, as do the signatures of younger men—Curzon, Asquith and Winston Churchill, whose fame, in the Baron's day, still lay before them.

On some occasions, it seems, Baron Ferdinand may have assumed the role of peace-maker when political acrimony was particularly rife. Under different administrations one finds the foremost members of the Opposition being invited to meet the leading Ministers of the day. These were often preceded by, or accompanied by their closest collaborators—Permanent Secretaries and Private Secretaries. Many diplomats figure prominently, particularly when the countries to which they were accredited were of topical concern. Often, however, there was an unexpected mixture of guests, as, for instance, in August 1886, when one finds the Archbishop of Canterbury being invited to meet the Speaker and the German and Austrian Ambassadors. What, one wonders, did they discuss? Or did they just enjoy each other's company?

Very often, however, one can at least imagine the subject of some of the conversations held in the Waddesdon dining-room or billiard room. It is remarkable how many people appeared to come to stay at Waddesdon immediately after they had taken part in some notable event. As an instance, Lord Wolseley, on reaching this country after the capture of Khartoum, headed straight for Waddesdon, as did British Ambassadors after important international conferences, or war-correspondents, hot-foot from some Balkan war. It seems more than likely that Baron Ferdinand delighted in having such interesting people to stay and enjoyed being one of the best informed of men, but he may, perhaps, have had an additional reason for seeking to acquire up-to-date knowledge from the eye-witnesses of important happenings.

For many years he had been a friend of the Prince of Wales, who had first been accustomed to stay with him while the Baron was still living at Leighton House. The Prince was a regular guest at Waddesdon from the moment it became habitable. Sir Sidney Lee, in his official biography of King Edward VII, describes in detail the Prince's many attempts to persuade his mother to allow him to see Cabinet and Foreign Office papers and thus have some inside knowledge of the events which he thought were the rightful concern of the Heir-Apparent. For many years, however, the Queen invariably refused these requests and indeed ordered her Ministers to deny any pleas for information they might receive from the Prince, on the grounds that his discretion was not to be trusted. The Prince's sense of political responsibility and consuming interest in international affairs did not allow him to let the matter rest there and

it is known that he made every attempt to keep himself as well informed as possible, despite his mother's ban. It indeed seems likely that Baron Ferdinand was one of the people through whom the Prince acquired some of the information he longed for and, if the Baron acted, in many instances, as the Prince's ears and eyes this may explain the presence of some of the guests at Waddesdon and the celerity with which they made their way there from foreign parts and interesting events.

The majority of those who came to Waddesdon had predominantly political interests but some of Baron Ferdinand's visitors were more concerned with the arts than with public affairs. Writers, ranging from Guy de Maupassant, Henry James and Paul Bourget to Mrs Humphrey Ward came to stay, as did painters, sculptors and musicians. Although in almost all Baron Ferdinand's house-parties the men outnumbered the women, the latter included many of those who exerted some influence on society through their beauty and their charm, but maybe sometimes through their brains. Lady Warwick, Lady de Grey and Lady Randolph Churchill were frequent guests as were Lady Dorothy Nevill, Lady Helen Vincent and Louise, Duchess of Manchester. The last, after her second marriage, gave the

43

Baron Ferdinand at the
Devonshire House fancy
dress ball, 1897

The Prince of Wales playing
tennis

famous fancy dress ball at Devonshire House in the year of the
Diamond Jubilee, and is thus indirectly responsible for those
yellowing photographs which can be found in so many great
houses in which *fin-de-siècle* ladies and gentlemen are implau-
sibly portrayed as Arthurian knights, Queens of the Nile and
Renaissance courtiers.

In 1889 the Shah of Persia was visiting this country and
was proving to be a somewhat awkward guest to entertain. The
Prince of Wales persuaded Baron Ferdinand to invite the Shah
to stay at Waddesdon, with his numerous suite, but at the same
time warned the Baron that he would not be able to come
himself. In place of his own invaluable presence on this rather
unnerving occasion, the Prince offered his two young sons, the
Duke of Clarence and Prince George (later King George V) who
told me, many years later, how clearly he remembered this
unusual party. He said that it got off to a poor start. On his
arrival the Shah was told that the Prince of Wales would not
be coming and this so displeased him that he went to the
bedroom prepared for him and stayed there, refusing to come
down to dinner. After a somewhat agitated discussion between
Baron Ferdinand and his other guests, a message was

Lady Randolph Churchill dressed as Cleopatra for the Devonshire House fancy dress ball, 1897

Tea on the North lawn at Waddesdon with the Prince of Wales

conveyed to the Shah that—as it happened—a most excellent conjurer had been engaged to entertain him after he had dined. This bait proved successful; the Shah agreed to descend, and from that moment enjoyed the evening with gusto.

Entertaining more ordinary guests, even in a house as well equipped as Baron Ferdinand's, was not always free from pre-occupation and the Baron was obviously of a temperament to which order and due warning were dear. Lady de Grey, writing to a friend, urged her to lose no time in making up her mind about whether to accept an invitation to Waddesdon. 'You know how funny Ferdy is' wrote Lady de Grey, 'he always likes an early answer'.

The time at which guests would arrive or depart was also a matter of natural concern to the Baron. We who are used to guests appearing driving their own motors, and leaving equally effortlessly, can have little idea of the complications of arranging the transport of up to 24 guests who could approach only via the railway station where a variety of different trains had to be met or caught by means of horse-drawn carriages. Moreover, many of Baron Ferdinand's guests, unlike ours, were not bound to be back at their office desks at nine o'clock on Monday morning, and the length of time any one of them might

decide to stay was not always a foregone conclusion. This may explain a story told me by someone who had once, rather nervously, arrived for the first time at Waddesdon. Having been greeted by the Baron, his composure was in no way increased when he was then immediately asked 'When are you leaving?'. It took him some time to realise that this question had only been put so that the necessary orders could go to the stables; not through any oversight of his would the Baron be guilty of incommoding a guest.

But of all the occasions on which the Baron planned and plotted to meet his visitors' wishes, probably none gave him more cause for thought than the visit of Queen Victoria who came to Waddesdon for the day in May, 1890. Having lived in seclusion at Osborne and in Scotland for so many years, the news, when it became known, that the Queen might be visible to some of her subjects in Buckinghamshire when she passed through Aylesbury on her way to Waddesdon, was greeted almost with unbelief, but unbounded enthusiasm. The arrangements made for what was, after all, a private luncheon party, are so unusual from our modern standpoint, that I find Baron Ferdinand's own account of this day enthralling. In the hope that it may be of interest to others as well as to myself, here is his account in full:

'In November 1888 the Empress Frederick invited me to an audience at Windsor Castle. When our conversation which had ranged over a diversity of interesting topics had lasted for an hour, the clock pointed to luncheon time and I prepared to withdraw. As I was taking my leave, the Empress announced to me, somewhat to my surprise, that the Queen had requested her to apprise me of her intention to honour me with a visit to Waddesdon in the course of the following Spring. The visit, however, although all the preliminaries had been settled during the month of April, failed to come off as the Princess Beatrice, who was expecting her confinement, and by whom the Queen wished to be accompanied, was not in a condition to undertake the journey. When dining at Windsor in the summer of that year, Her Majesty's first words to me were that she had not forgotten her intention of honouring me with her presence at Waddesdon, and that she fully intended carrying it out in the following year.

On the 12th of April of this year, I duly received a letter from Sir Henry Ponsonby at Aix-les-Bains, where he was in attendance on Her Majesty, stating that the Queen proposed visiting me at Waddesdon on the 14th, 15th or

16th of May. A lengthy and detailed correspondence ensued, and the visit was ultimately fixed for Wednesday, May 14th. For some considerable time, the best part of my day was employed in exchanging notes and telegrams with Sir Henry Ponsonby; settling the hours of Her Majesty's departure from and arrival at Windsor and Waddesdon respectively; the list of the guests, the number of the carriages and the servants, and last but not least, the etiquette that was to be observed on the occasion. With the one solitary exception of declining an escort of the Royal Bucks Yeomanry, which I can only attribute to her objections to the indifferent horsemanship usually displayed by Her Majesty's auxiliary forces—though from personal experience I can say that the Bucks force form a brilliant exception to the general rule in that respect—the Queen acceded to every one of my suggestions and evinced the most gracious willingness to facilitate my programme of arrangements.

Princess Louise exhibited much kindness also in aiding me with her advice, and in recommending to Her Majesty's acceptance my proposals which, indeed, were framed entirely with a view to Her Majesty's convenience.

Princess Louise, and the majority of the other guests arrived at Waddesdon on Tuesday the 13th of May. The weather was cloudy and cold and the glass was falling. Perhaps a barometer has rarely been consulted so often or so anxiously as that at Waddesdon on the day preceding Her Majesty's visit. As the Queen had never been—at any rate since her accession to the throne—in that part of Buckinghamshire in which I reside, the loyalty, curiosity and enthusiasm of the population were raised to the highest pitch by the prospect of her coming. In the small town of Aylesbury, upwards of three hundred pounds were subscribed for stands and decorations. At Fleet Marston, about half way between Aylesbury and the entrance lodge to my park, I also erected a stand, mainly for the accommodation of the tenants of some of my relatives and friends; and another at the Waddesdon Cross Roads, for my own tenants and for the inhabitants of the villages situated on my estate, while there was, of course, the usual triumphal arch.

On Wednesday morning at eleven o'clock, I left the house for the railway station, meeting on the road Lord Hartington and the Granbys who had come that morning from London to join the party at Waddesdon. The glass, meantime, had done its duty and a more perfect day for the visit, or one better suited to the Queen's peculiar taste, could not be imagined. A brilliant sun shone from a perfectly blue sky, a crisp, cold wind tempered the atmosphere, and the dust had been laid by the rain so that we could dispense with the use of watering carts.

At the station I found Lord Rothschild, exercising on this occasion, for the first time, the official functions as Lord Lieutenant of the county. Punctually at ten minutes past twelve the Royal train steamed in to the platform, and and I was amused to notice a gaudily painted crown and cushion of iron had been placed at the base of the funnel to indicate the rank of its chief passenger. The Queen was seated in a saloon carriage, together with her daughter and son-in-law, reading the morning papers. The weather, as usual, served to initiate the conversation, but the words attributed to Her Majesty in the press, that 'I always bring fine weather with me' are not accurate. Something of that kind was said *by me*, but the Queen, instead of accepting for herself a royal influence over the elements, merely uttered a few words, which I cannot precisely recollect, but which consisted of an allusion to the wilfulness of the climate and the fortunate change the weather had undergone that morning.

To compare the decorations of Aylesbury, or the crowds provided by its nine thousand inhabitants, with those of great cities of the country on the occasion of other royal visits, would of course be absurd. But still I may say that considering the circumstances of the place, the aspect of this small country town and the spontaneous outburst of enthusiasm which greeted the procession on its way through it, were altogether out of the common; the whole scene, quite mediaeval in its picturesqueness, was stirring and effective in the utmost degree. Taste in pageantry is not, as a rule, characteristic of English country people, but whether the irregularity of the streets and buildings lent itself to the purposes of decoration or owing to a fortunate accident in the selection of the sites for decorations, so that they disguised the natural blemishes of the place while bringing into relief its quaint features, or because of the richness and profusion of the arches, banners and flags which, having been used for the Jubilee in London were cheaply obtained—from whatever reason, the general effect was most happy. We went through the town at a foot's pace, where the inevitable address was presented by Major Horwood of the Volunteers, Chairman of the Board of Health, at the foot of the steps of the Town Hall, while

Watercolour of Waddesdon painted by Miss Alice's governess and life-long friend, Mademoiselle Cécile Hofer.

48

Waddesdon 1885.

the equally inevitable bouquet was presented to the Queen by his daughter, Miss Horwood. The Queen's carriage led the way in the procession, preceded by Her Majesty's outriders; Lady Errol, Lady Ponsonby, Lord Rothschild and myself followed in a landau and four; Sir Henry Ponsonby and Miss Phipps coming next in a Victoria, and behind them came in a wagonette one of the Queen's Indian servants, a footman and a dresser. On reaching the Cross Roads my carriage left the procession and trotted on through the village so that I might be at the house to meet the Queen, who drove through the park. There I duly waited to receive Her Majesty together with my sister, Princess Louise and the members of my family, while the other guests were, by command, locked up in the adjacent drawingrooms.

When the Queen descended from her carriage, my sister conducted her at once to the Small Library on the ground floor, which had been transformed into a dressing-room for the occasion. Shortly after, the Royal Party entered the large Dining Room where luncheon was served to them; upon which the guests were released from their confinement and lunched with me in the Small Dining Room, while the Royal Artillery Band, which was stationed in the small conservatory which connects the two rooms, played a selection of airs. The royal appetite is proverbial, and it was not until about half past three that the Queen and her daughters re-appeared in the Red Drawing Room. Evidently my cook had done his duty, for, as I was afterwards informed by my butler, Her Majesty partook of every dish and twice of cold beef. As a further evidence of her approval of the good things provided for her, I may mention that she took away three copies of the bill of fare, and that the Royal Cook was subsequently sent to learn from mine, the secret of making three of the dishes which had been sent up. The Queen, though in black, wearing her widow's cap, which she had assumed before luncheon instead of her bonnet, was nevertheless smartly dressed, and wore various brooches and lockets containing miniatures, one of which seemed to me to be a likeness of the Princess Alice.

At last the expectant guests were allowed to sun themselves in the Royal smile, but their conversational powers were not severely taxed, as Her Majesty was only pleased to address a few stereotyped sentences to those of them with whom she was better acquainted, while those whom I had to present, had to rest satisfied with a gracious smile.

The Red Drawing Room. On the right is Gainsborough's portrait of George IV when Prince of Wales. Reflected in the looking glass over the fireplace is the same artist's portrait of Lady Sheffield.

49

Looking towards the
conservatory from the
breakfast room

I had been informed that I was not to show too much zeal
in displaying my property to the Queen, so as not to tire
her. The hint was unnecessary, as I never intended to have
taken her through any of the rooms except those known as
my own apartment. Her Majesty looked with interest on the
old English portraits in my Green sitting room, and at some
of the curiosities in the Tower Room; and was so struck
with the decoration, furnishing and arrangement of the
rooms that she afterwards sent the superintendent of the
furniture from Windsor Castle to inspect them. She gave
proof of her memory and knowledge of genealogies when
I showed her a large miniature picture, representing my
Grandfather and Grandmother with their seven children,
with whose intricate relationship and marriages she was
thoroughly conversant. She told me that she particularly
remembered my Grandfather, and on my expressing some
surprise, seeing that he died in 1836, she said, with one

50

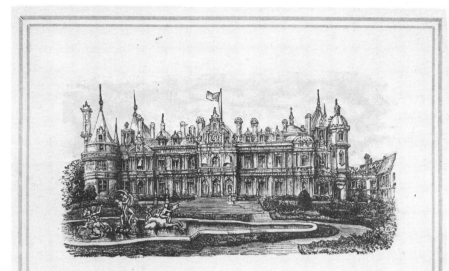

DÉJEÛNER DE SA MAJESTÉ
LA REINE.

Potage.
Comsommé à la Windsor.

Poisson.
Truite à la Norwégienne.

Entrées.
Cailles en Caisses.

Poularde à l'Algérienne.

Relevé.
Filets de Bœuf à la Chartreuse.

Rôt.
Canetons Garnis d'Ortolans.

Entremets.
Asperges en Branches.

Beignets à la Viennoise.

Petites Soufflés à la Royale.

A mis-spelled 'proof copy'
(the only one to remain) of
the menu of the luncheon
for Queen Victoria

Baron Ferdinand's own sitting room (now known as the 'Baron's Room') in which he surrounded himself with pictures of pretty women. The two pictures to the left are by Reynolds (Perdita Robinson and Mrs Scott of Danesfield), on the right Mrs Jordan by Romney

of those charming smiles of which no one has the secret better than Her Majesty and her children, 'Why not? I was then eighteen years of age'.

After dinner rest awhile says the old proverb, and it evidently holds good in all ranks of society. The suite of rooms known as the State Apartments, on the bedroom floor, had been got in readiness in the event of the Queen wishing to seclude herself from the profane gaze. I conducted her upstairs, and in spite of the rheumatic affection of the knee from which she suffers, Her Majesty ascended the long flight with comparative ease. I then left her in the State Apartments, and during her absence smoked a cigar on the Terrace with Prince Henry of Battenberg, but had to throw away the fragrant weed unfinished, being bitterly railed at by my relations who said I should be reeking of smoke when Her Majesty came down.

On the previous day, a German curiosity dealer had been down to see the house bringing with him various things for my inspection, among them a diminutive French ivory fan of the last century, most beautifully set in diamonds. A more appropriate offering to the Queen could not have been desired so I begged Princess Louise to ask Her Majesty whether she would be pleased to accept it from me as a memento of her visit. At four o'clock I was sent for by Her Majesty to receive the fan. Were I of a shy disposition, a more embarrassing situation could hardly have been provided for me. The Queen was standing in the Small Green Boudoir—which I may incidentally mention I purchased some years ago in the rue de Richelieu at the Marshal de Richelieu's former residence, number 27—looking very majestic, solemn and severe; flanked on either side by her two daughters who seemed rather curious to observe how I should acquit myself of my task. But being neither shy nor embarrassed, I delivered a harangue worthy of an Elizabethan courtier, and having received the Queen's acceptance of the present, I knelt on one knee and handed it to her. It clearly gave much pleasure to Her Majesty as I could infer from the fact that, on my remarking that the initials of the lady for whom the fan had been made should be erased and replaced by those of Her Majesty, she seemed reluctant to part with it and replied that it would do very well as it was. I then bowed myself out of the room; and after an interval of a quarter of an hour, during which time Her Majesty's cap was re-exchanged for her bonnet, I was informed that she was ready to inspect the grounds.

The Queen's little pony-carriage had been sent down on the previous day to my stables. It is really like a bath-chair, and is drawn by a little pony which, as the Queen informed me, had first seen the light in the New Forest. The reins lay idly in Her Majesty's lap, while the bit was secured in the firm grip of one of the Queen's Highlanders, a brother of the deceased John Brown. I had ordered various pony-traps and carriages for the rest of the company; some of them, however, preferred following us on foot. We made at once for the Aviary, but the Queen's attention was diverted from its gaily feathered inhabitants by the conduct of her pony, which shied at the sight of the cockatoos and macaws which screamed and flapped their wings on their perches in the centre of the grass plot in front of the Aviary. The poor birds, however, meant no harm and were merely asking me for their usual piece of sugar. We next proceeded to one of the adjacent lawns, where my bailiff, Sims, and his foreman were ready for the fulfilment of the time-honoured custom of planting the tree—for which purpose a *Picea concolor* had been selected. I may observe that when, on the preceding day, I was on my way to Aylesbury to meet Princess Louise, I passed a dog-cart and my attention was involuntarily arrested by some-thing peculiar in the appearance of the person who was sitting next to the driver. I had been requested to allow an artist from the *Illustrated London News* to take sketches of the proceedings at Waddesdon during the Royal visit, and my instinct told me that the gentleman in the dogcart was the artist in question. I was not mistaken, for after our carriages had crossed, feeling impelled me to turn round and I saw that the dogcart had stopped and that the gentleman was violently gesticulating to me to do the same. I did so and he entered my carriage, at once putting a series of questions to me as to how he could take sketches of the various incidents of the following day. I said to

Queen Victoria planting a tree at Waddesdon in May, 1890

The spade with which this act was performed

him—'You are quite at liberty to sketch any scenes you like, provided you do not permit yourself to be noticed'. 'Oh sir', he replied in a tone and manner the peculiar cockney vulgarity of which cannot possibly be reproduced—'I have been following the Queen about for ever so many years, and know exactly what I am to do. Where is the Queen going to plant the tree?' he enquired to my amusement. 'On one of the lawns' I answered, 'Why do you ask?'. 'Because', said he, 'I want to select a bush from behind which I can sketch the ceremony without being seen'. While the Queen was planting the tree, I could not refrain from investigating the shrubberies and there was the artist esconced behind a *Thuja gigantea*, adjusting the focus of a photographic apparatus on the *Picea concolor* and the august lady who was handling the spade. The tree planting ceremony over, we passed the deer pen which contains an Indian Black Buck, and Her Majesty was much pleased to behold a denizen of her Indian Empire. From thence we proceeded past the stables to the glass houses and I took advantage of the favourable opportunity then afforded me, of conversing quietly with the Queen, unheard by strangers, and broached subjects altogether irrelevant to the situation. The Queen entered freely into the conversation and I regret being too indolent to use my own pen, and unwilling to dictate the substance of our interview, the readers—if any readers there will ever be of this paper—will be debarred from learning its import. So much only can I say, that the various statesmen not only of Great Britain but of Europe, were freely canvassed.

Some of the flowering shrubs attracted a good deal of attention from the Queen, and she greatly admired the varieties of gorse and broom and a Japanese crabtree. So much so indeed, that my sister since received a note from Miss Phipps, asking for the exact botanical names of those plants. Mr Sander, the St Albans orchid grower, was in readiness at the entrance to the glasshouses, and I presented him to the Queen who addressed a few words to him, but he was so shy that he was unable to answer, and would have bolted straight away had I not held him back by the coat-tails. Sander was the only one of the many professionals I had employed in the creation of the estate selected for presentation to the Queen, an honour which he highly prized as he took good care to have it duly recorded and advertised in the press. I may mention that not only Sander but my butler and cook copiously dosed with champagne the *Daily Telegraph* reporter to whom I had given permission to come to Waddesdon, to secure their being mentioned in his report of the proceedings of the day. My poor gardener, to whom the opportunity was not afforded of plying the reporter with the same generous vintage, was ignominiously left out in the cold; and even the bouquet which I presented to the Queen—the work of his hands, and a more beautiful bouquet I have never seen, consisting of vandateres with sprays of odontoglossum pescatori—was described in the newspapers as having been made by Sander himself. *Surtout pas trop de zèle*, the words addressed by Talleyrand to one of his underlings, should have been remembered by my gardener, who was so anxious that the plants entrusted to his care should be duly appreciated, that he opened the doors of the stovehouses leading into the central corridor, instead of keeping them closed, which would not have prevented us from admiring the plants through the large glass panels of the doors, while keeping the heat from the central corridor, which, as it was, was so intense that we had to rush through it. The atmosphere of the orchid ranges was more endurable, where, oddly enough, the comparatively insignificant cyprepedium caudatum excited the greatest admiration from the Queen and her daughters. On concluding the inspection of the glass, the Queen re-entered her pony-carriage, we wended our way slowly up the hill homewards, and again I had the advantage of conversing with the Queen on matters highly interesting to myself. I left Her Majesty in the oriental tent on the tennis lawn in front of the house, where she partook of tea in the company of her family and my sister. About a quarter after five the Queen returned to the house, and having attended to her toilette in the small dressing room, she took her leave of the company. I shall never forget the manner in which the Queen bowed herself out of the house. The guests were assembled round the oval vestibule inside the front door: the Queen stood alone on the doorstep, and curtsied to the company in the most dignified and graceful manner— a marvellous performance. The procession returned to Aylesbury in the same order as it had driven thence. The stands along the road and at Aylesbury were, perhaps, somewhat less crowded than they had been in the morning, but the enthusiasm was as great as before. At the station, Her Majesty gave me her hand to kiss and made a few remarks expressive of the satisfaction she had derived from the visit—of which she gave further proof, subsequently, by presenting me with a small marble bust of herself by

Queen Victoria leaving
Waddesdon

Boehm, with an appropriate inscription on the pedestal. The train steamed off, my cousin and myself drove home, thoroughly exhausted, but delighted that the visit had come to an end, and above all, that it had passed off so satisfactorily.

The result may be considered eminently agreeable in every sense of the word. That the Sovereign of this realm who, for the last thirty years, has lived in almost complete privacy, should have found my house an attraction so exceptional as to draw her from her seclusion, was highly gratifying to myself; but that gratification was enhanced by the fact that the Queen, as I have been informed by the Prince of Wales and every member of her household I have since seen, was thoroughly delighted with the arrangements I had made for her comfort, and with the place itself. That she lunched alone with members of her family, instead of lunching with us, has been commented on in society—but without reason. The proposal that she should do so emanated from me, as I was well aware, not only of her disinclination to take her midday meal in the company of strangers, but of the invariable rule, which she never breaks, of so doing.

Around the Queen of England there hangs an undefinable prestige, the result of a long and glorious reign; of singular domestic virtue; of an unblemished fame; of great political sagacity and unique simplicity of character on the one hand, and a supreme queenly dignity on the other. She, alone of all the Sovereigns of Europe, combines the charm of a woman with a legitimate consciousness of her position, and while ever ready to sympathise with the humble of her subjects and even to forget her position and her cares in the company of her chosen friends, maintains whenever she is called upon to do so, the most striking dignity. Her conversation may be sparse and her dress old-fashioned, but every word she utters bears witness to the fact that she is a lady in the true sense of the word, and her every attitude, whether walking, driving or sitting, is that of the first lady of the land.

This is all the more telling when we compare her with the other sovereigns of Europe and their consorts. The Emperor of Russia has only distinguished himself by his intolerance, his bigotry, his inaccessibility and his invincible objection to promoting any beneficial measures for

Baron Ferdinand in his sitting room with his dog 'Poupon'

his empire; while the Empress of Russia is only known to the outer world for her fondness of dress, and her daily increasing profusion of jewels. The Emperor of Germany is a clever young man, no doubt, but is a nineteenth century Hohenzollern, a restless fidget, a combination of autocrat and socialist, a German dreamer on the one hand, and an embryo Napoleon on the other: while his wife has only signalised herself by giving birth to a large family, by her tea-parties and her embroideries, her mystic aspirations and the almost countless number of her suite. The Emperor of Austria, a Hapsburg of the old school, is a well-meaning monarch, but narrow-minded in every sense of the term. During his long reign of forty-two years, his army has been beaten by that of almost every European country, and the laurels, borne by his effigy on his coins, were only won by his victory over his own Hungarian subjects in 1848. He may rise at five in the morning and work until five in the afternoon, and be animated by the most laudable intentions, but it would be better if he worked less and thought more—or at any rate, more intelligently. The King of Italy is a man, a soldier and a king, while his wife was

Writing table presented to Beaumarchais by his friends in 1781

once a very pretty woman and knows how to maintain her position. But, absurd as it may appear, for the King of Italy is a descendant of an old and illustrious house, Italy is but an upstart kingdom and its sovereign is not regarded as having the same prestige as his royal contemporaries, while his kingdom is honeycombed with revolutionary societies and undermined with revolutionary principles, and an Italian Republic may not be in the far distant future. It would be superfluous to mention the other minor sovereigns of Europe, most of whom are mere vassals or dependants of their greater neighbours, many of whose brothers and children marry actresses and dancers and who spend their time in going about from one continental country to another in first class carriages, dining in French cafés, and simply leading the lives of prosperous or adventurous citizens. Long may the Queen of England live for the benefit of the institutions, the security and satisfaction of her subjects! The day may may come when the Crown of Great Britain may be exchanged for the Phrygian Cap. May I not live to see it. From the political, as well as the social point of view, the results of the change could be but deplorable.

With the expression of these sentiments, I shall conclude this paper. Into whose hands will it fall? Who will be its first reader, and by whom will it be first opened? And will the thoughts and descriptions I have jotted down, afford him or her satisfaction or the reverse? Things to which we, the contemporaries of an event, whether significant or insignificant, attach importance, are nearly always viewed in a different light by future generations, and what may interest us may not interest them. I cannot look into the future, and in fact have only consigned to paper my thoughts on the Queen's visit to Waddesdon, not for any special reasons of my own, or for the gratification of my vanity, but because I have been pressed by my numerous friends to keep a record of an event, which in days far forward, may be regarded as one of some significance, and likely to arouse the historical, archaeological and social curiosity of unborn generations.'

The Prince of Wales' last visit to Waddesdon before Baron Ferdinand died did not end as satisfactorily as the Queen's. The Prince, one Monday morning in July, 1898, intent on having breakfast before catching a train to Windsor, left his bedroom and came down the West Stairs. Lord Warwick, who was also staying in the house, described what happened next in his 'Memoirs of Sixty Years'. He wrote:

Opposite One of the eighteenth century bindings of books by Padeloup collected by Baron Ferdinand

Overleaf Three of the bookplates in Baron Ferdinand's collection

Binding by Le Gascon, 1641

60

Bibl. Hug
de Bassville

Rendés le livre s'il vous plait.

DE LA BIBLIOTHÈQUE,
DE M. LAVOISIER,
de L'Academie Royale des Sciences,
regisseur des Poudres et Salpêtres
de France, E.ur General du Roy.

De la Gardette fecit

DULCES ANTE OMNIA MUSÆ.

DEUS NOBIS HÆC OTIA FECIT.

C. S. IORDANI, ET AMICORUM.

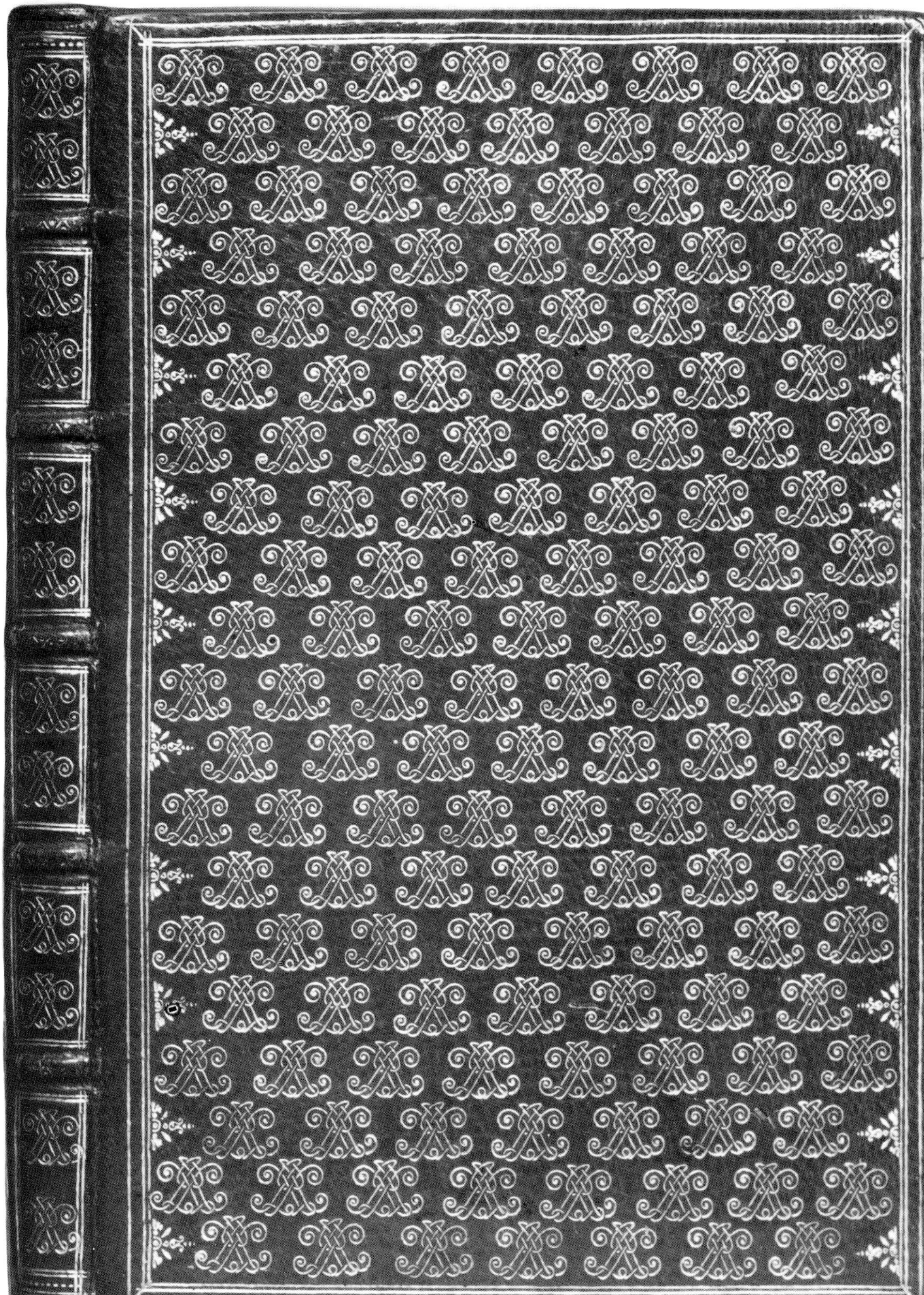

'I was out early and sitting on a chair in front of the house talking to one of the guests—I can't remember to whom. Suddenly the butler came out and asked anxiously if I knew where the Baron was. I replied I had not yet seen him, and asked if anything was amiss, as the poor man was greatly agitated. 'I fear' he replied, 'that the Prince of Wales has met with a bad accident. He slipped heavily on the spiral staircase, and is now sitting down there unable to move'. I hurried into the house, and found the Prince where the butler had left him, sitting on a step of the main circular staircase. He smiled re-assuringly at me, although I could see at a glance that he must be in great pain, and said: 'I fear I have broken something in my leg; my foot slipped, and as I fell I heard a bone crack'. Two servants came up at that moment bearing a long invalid chair, and fearing from what the Prince had said that he had split or broken his knee-cap, I tied his leg straight out onto one of the parallel carrying poles. Then the local doctor arrived, and the Prince was allowed to sit on a sofa with his leg down, to have his breakfast before leaving. I have always thought that but for the severe strain involved by his straightened leg the subsequent illness would not have been so long or so difficult—but I will not blame the doctor. The Prince was ever the kindliest of men, and his great anxiety was to reassure Baron Ferdinand, who was so grieved to think he should have met with a serious accident under his roof'.

Many years later, the Royal Bucks Hospital in Aylesbury began to wonder why they were 'Royal' and asked me if I could tell them whether they had received that distinctive title because the Prince of Wales had been taken there after breaking his leg at Waddesdon. I was almost sure that I had been told that the Prince had insisted on being taken straight back to Windsor, but I thought, before giving an answer it might be as well to check my memory. My investigations revealed an even more disastrous ending to the Prince's visit than that recorded by Lord Warwick. It appears the Prince was placed in a carriage at Waddesdon, with the carrying-chair, and driven to Aylesbury station. Then, as now, if one wishes to take a train from Aylesbury to Windsor the right platform can only be reached by traversing a high bridge over the rails which is approached, at either end, by steep turning stairs. The Prince, now a big heavy man of nearly sixty years of age, was safely carried from the carriage, into the station and up the stairs on to the bridge. But then his weight became too much for the carrying chair. It broke, depositing him unceremoniously and most painfully

The Grey Drawing Room. The portrait in the corner is of Lady Jane Halliday by Reynolds. The Savonnerie carpet was woven on a design by P.-J. Perrot for the dining room of Louis XV at the Grand Trianon in 1745.

in the middle of the bridge which from time to time, was engulfed by the acrid smoke of trains passing underneath it. It is hard to imagine how the Prince was eventually got off the bridge and into the Windsor train; doubtless, there were many willing hands, including Baron Ferdinand's, but it seems likely that the extra agony this final accident caused may have been just as responsible as the Waddesdon doctor's treatment—which Lord Warwick so doubted—for making the Prince's leg take so long to mend.

Baron Ferdinand died very suddenly in his bath, at Waddesdon, from a heart attack, on his 59th birthday. When the news of his death became known the Bucks County Council suspended its sitting and directed that a flag should be flown at half mast from the County Hall; the drivers of the hansom cabs and growlers which plied for hire in Piccadilly tied black ribbons to their whips and the Prince of Wales attended the memorial Service in the Central Synagogue which was held on the day Baron Ferdinand was buried beside his beloved wife in the Jewish Cemetry at West Ham.

His death in 1898 cut short the life of a man who still had much to contribute to the country of his adoption in the cultural, charitable and political fields. At Waddesdon his prediction that others might reap the chief benefit of his labour of love proved to be tragically accurate. He was widely loved, both in his family circle and by many friends in all walks of life. I think it was the fashion of the day for newspapers to print obituaries of length, giving complete details of every phase of their subject's life, but when, many years later, I found two huge volumes of cuttings from newspapers, of every shade of opinion and nationality, eulogising Baron Ferdinand for all he did and all he was, I could not help feeling that he must have been a most exceptional human being. To quote from one paper: 'Beneficence had been the business of his life'.

By his Will he left the contents of his London house in Piccadilly to relatives and friends. He bequeathed his collection of Renaissance objects in what he termed his 'new smoking room' at Waddesdon to the British Museum;* he made large bequests to hospitals and charities, particularly those concerned with the welfare of merchant seamen and their dependants, and, after making handsome provision for all those who had worked for him in Buckinghamshire and elsewhere, he left the Waddesdon estate to his sister, Alice.

A writing table inlaid with Sèvres plaques which was made by Martin Carlin in 1766.

* Where they are known as The Waddesdon Bequest. By order of the Trustees they have recently been beautifully re-arranged in a room of their own by Mr. Hugh Tait, who is also compiling a new and detailed catalogue of this bequest.

Miss Alice
1847-1922

BARON FERDINAND'S BEQUEST of Waddesdon to his sister may have caused some surprise. After all, it was only shortly before the Baron's death that Lord Meath, in the House of Lords, had had the temerity to recommend that the law should be changed so as to allow women to be elected to County Councils, on which, he thought, they might be helpful in such matters as the boarding-out of children. Although Lord Meath was instant to point out to their Lordships that he would utterly deprecate his proposal being used as the thin edge of any wedge which might one day enable ladies to sit at Westminster, (plainly, he said, they would be incapable of dealing with matters of *haute politique*) his suggestion was considered so foolish that he was quite unable to find another peer to second him.

The inheritance of Waddesdon was, of course, an entirely private family affair, but in the prevailing opinion of the day it seems that an estate of this kind was thought to call for a capacity in its owner which was judged to be the prerogative of the male sex alone. Miss Alice, grieving deeply for her brother, may well have felt daunted, but I am sure that no one who knew her at all well could have doubted the intelligence, humanity and administrative ability which would enable her to succeed him. The record shows she was well up to her task.

Miss Alice, the youngest of Baron Anselm's seven surviving children, was born in Frankfort in 1847. She spent her early childhood in Vienna to which her father had been sent to take charge of the family banking business in Austria. Even as a small child she must have had something about her. When she was eight years old, her grandfather died and, in the habit of the day, the entire family were gathered together to learn his testamentary dispositions. The way in which he had left his house, the Grüneburg and its large park, on the outskirts of Frankfort, must have been a matter of personal interest and conjecture not only to Miss Alice's father, but also to her three brothers. But when the Will was read it was learnt, to the

Miss Alice de Rothschild (1847–1922) in her early twenties

67

Lady Battersea (1843–1931)

bemused surprise of everyone, that he had bequeathed the Grüneburg, in its entirety, to Miss Alice.

When she was twelve years old her mother died, and she went to live in the Grüneburg with her much older sister, Mathilde who, like so many of the family, had married a Rothschild cousin—the Baron Willy. Lady Battersea, an English relative, writing of Miss Alice, described her at this time. She said: ' She spent rather a lonely childhood, owing to the fact of her being the junior member of the family. Following a suggestion of her English cousins, during a visit of their's to Frankfort, she came to England in the late summer of 1860, with her French governess, Mademoiselle Hofer, who became her lifelong friend, and proceeded on a visit to her aunt, Lady de Rothschild. There, under the auspices of that beloved aunt she first learnt what country life and its duties implied. It was a happy time for the young motherless girl who shared a schoolroom existence with her cousins, soon to become her devoted friends. At that early age she already gave proof of very remarkable gifts, both mental and physical; indeed, her power of grasping the threads of an argument and of logical reasoning were unusual enough in one of her years to have aroused the admiration and astonishment of no less a personage than Matthew Arnold, who met her when staying at Aston Clinton as a guest of Lady de Rothschild. Alice was very proficient in all games of dexterity and skill; she was passionately fond of riding, and became as the years went on a fearless and well-known horsewoman. She always avowed that her visits to Aston Clinton had in a way prepared her for the great change that was about to come into her life '.

That change came when, having sold the Grüneburg to her sister and brother-in-law, the Baron and Baroness Willy, she determined to come to England permanently to be with her bereaved brother Ferdinand.

With Mademoiselle Hofer still at her side, she came to London and spent much of the winters with her brother at Leighton House. Here, as in London, Lady Battersea notes ' she proved a capable hostess to his many distinguished guests '—not an entirely easy thing to be at the age of 20 in what was still, to her, a foreign land. But she was determined not to be a foreigner for long and, in the following year, on reaching her majority, she became a naturalised British subject.

As the years went by she acquired—perhaps under her brother's influence—a great knowledge of works of art and showed a distinctive taste in their collection and arrangement. Miss Alice, I believe, may well have expressed her own ideas about the house her brother was planning to build and furnish

68

Miss Alice's elder sister, Mathilde, who married Baron Willy von Rothschild

at Waddesdon and possibly her ideas did not always entirely coincide with his. In any case, with her brother's encouragement, in 1875 she bought the neighbouring property of Eythrope and there set about building her own little Waddesdon. Monsieur Destailleur, working for her brother, was not asked to design her house for her; instead she chose an English architect, George Devey.

Eythrope had had a chequered history. It was an ancient property, first of the Dormers, then of the Stanhopes before it passed by descent to a French family, the d'Harcourts. It is said that the last Stanhope owner, being childless, sent for his French nephew and told him he would leave him the large house at Eythrope—with its renowned picture gallery—if he would promise him two things—that he would become a Protestant, and would spend six months of every year in England. The boy is said to have promised, but, the moment his Uncle was dead, reverted to the Catholic faith of his fathers, and never set foot in England again. At least it is true that for nearly a hundred years Eythrope House was uninhabited; then it was sold, not only the contents, but the fabric of the house itself, which was broken up into lots. It is said that Little Kimble church was built with material from Eythrope and that the very pretty front door of the County Museum in Aylesbury was once the door of Eythrope House. The d'Harcourts, however, retained possession of the land and it was from them that Miss Alice bought it, the only building then remaining being a ruined chapel which had once stood next to the vanished house.

Miss Alice decided not to build on the old foundations but

The Pavilion at Eythrope
from the air, with the river
in the foreground

instead set her new house a short distance away from them, in
the middle of a meadow bounded by the river Thame. As the
building of her house started Miss Alice fell ill—I imagine of
some form of rheumatic fever, a complaint which was to be-
devil her, on and off, for the rest of her days. Her doctor insisted,
in the medical fashion of the day, that damp at night-time was
the one thing she must avoid and told her that if she valued
her health she must never, never sleep at Eythrope; it was so
dangerously near water. This opinion must have been a severe
blow to Miss Alice, but she was not one to disregard advice
she considered expert. So Mr. Devey's plans were changed, and
the fairy-tale, towered, pink brick house, named the Pavilion,
was built to contain a sitting-room, a dining-room and a kitchen,
but *no* bedroom, so that she should never fall into the temptation

of sleeping there. The Pavilion was only four miles from Waddesdon and, in the following years, however many days Miss Alice spent at Eythrope, filling her house with works of art, organising her garden so that it should rival Waddesdon's, or entertaining her friends, she always returned to her brother's house at night.

An old acquaintance once described to me the usual routine of a summer day when visiting Waddesdon in the Baron's time. After a varied and leisurely breakfast a busy programme of inspection normally awaited his guests. The house-party might first descend the hill to the stables to admire or criticize the horses. Pausing, perhaps, to feed the Emus in their pen and braving the perfume of a grotto in which resided a mountain goat, they would then arrive at the glass-houses. Here they would wander through house after house of flowering exotic beauty. The Dairy was the next port of call, where those who wished to do so could sample the cream temptingly displayed in great bowls set out in a room embellished with decorative tiling. The Dairy 'Curio Room' would then be inspected. This housed Kändler models of Dresden animals and birds and ancient examples of faience and other curiosities which were then deemed 'rustic', but which are now thought to be some

The river Thame at Eythrope

The formal bedding on the
South terrace at Waddesdon
in Miss Alice's time

of Waddesdon's prize possessions. Toiling up the hill again
presumably gave the Baron's guests an appetite for luncheon.
Then, after a short rest, it would be time to go to Eythrope.
A long line of open landaus would draw up outside the front
door; Baron Ferdinand's guests would get in and, in a flurry
of parasols and panama hats, would go clip-clopping through
the park, over the road, and down through Miss Alice's
long avenue of chestnuts. Then, I am told, it all depended
on the weather, where they would have tea. If it was
overcast they would drive straight to the Pavilion, but if the
sun shone, they would transfer themselves into a large electric
launch, manned by boatmen in straw hats, banded with blue
and yellow ribbons—the family racing colours. Damp being
only distinctly dangerous at night, they would then glide up
the Thame to an enchanting tea-house Miss Alice had built on
the river at the farthest point of her property.

But the weather can change at a moment's notice in England, as we all know. I had an old friend at Waddesdon who had worked for the family for many years. One day I asked him what his first job had been and he described it to me with relish and enjoyment. He said, as a boy of 12, he had been the cake-holder. He explained that on cloudy days, the delectable tea provided at Eythrope for the approaching guests from Waddesdon, would be set out in the dining-room of the Pavilion. Then, just as the landaus were arriving, the weather might change, the sun would shine, and it was realised that the guests might prefer to go up river. Happily the Thame does not pursue a straight course through the meadows, but winds its way. This made it possible for the big iced cakes, the ginger-snaps and wafer-thin sandwiches to be whipped off the table and packed into a pony-trap. This would be driven by a colleague straight across the fields to the tea-house at a speed which would enable the tea to beat the approaching launch by a short head. My old friend's task had been to stand in the trap, poised over the cakes, keeping them from over-setting and their fragile icing from damage, as they careered over the rough ground. Angel cakes, he remembered, had been particularly volatile and apt to bounce. As he recalled those long-gone summer afternoons he implied that those, indeed, had been the days.

The terrace at Eythrope: Baron Ferdinand seated 2nd from left: Miss Alice standing, far right

Some of those for whom those teas were made have also left us their impressions. In 1897, that great civil servant, Sir Algernon West noted in his diary:* 'On the 5th June, at the height of its glory, I went to Ferdinand Rothschild's at Waddesdon, and on Sunday to Miss Alice de Rothschild's fairy garden at Eythrope, both lovely; the only possible criticism that could be made were that they were too perfect—if that is possible'. He went on to record 'At Waddesdon J. Chamberlain said Mr. Gladstone was a bad judge of men; that he saw no difference between Harcourt, Bright and Childers. From a high mountain all things look equal. Chamberlain contended that it was an impossibility to be great and good—in reference to Napoleon. The essence of goodness was to be unselfish and indeed self-denying and thus to destroy greatness. Walked with Haldane, who said Chamberlain had strong Liberal leanings. Thought Rosebery very wise to wait. Would form a party of his own: E. Grey Foreign Secretary. Asquith not progressing. Mrs. Asquith apt to sacrifice the future for the pleasure of to-day; the result of superabundance of animal vitality and spirit. . .'

The entrance corridor to the main part of the glasshouses

* *The Private Diaries of Sir Algernon West.* John Murray, 1922

These small vignettes provided by Sir Algernon of some of the leading personalities of the time give the flavour of the opinion-forming gossip at political house-parties in the last years of Queen Victoria's reign.

Miss Alice never married. When she received her great inheritance she was a maiden lady, aged 51. To quote Lady Battersea again: ' At Waddesdon her rule was a very determined if also a generous one. Gifted with intellect and a firm sense of duty, also an unusually strong power of will and inflexibility of purpose, she pursued her way of life, managing her property, looking after every detail of her estate, undeterred by any opposition she might meet with. For some years her face and figure were well known in the villages of the neighbourhood, for she would drive herself about in a low phaeton, drawn by two nimble little ponies. She never changed her style of dress summer or winter, that of a tailor-made suit in soft grey cloth, with old-fashioned collars and cuffs, and her head covered by a panama hat. Those who met her walking in her garden remarked that she always carried a spud in her hand, with which she removed any offending weed from the carefully kept paths. No

A horse-drawn mower on the cricket ground at Waddesdon: at the back, the Pavilion from the roof of which Baron Ferdinand used to address his constituents

Formal bedding at
Waddesdon

Opposite Miss Alice in old
age at Eythrope

The Smoking room corridor
hung with small arms
collected by Miss Alice to
replace some of the objects
left by her brother to the
British Museum

freaks or changes of fashion worried or affected her. She had
never been good-looking, but had keen, bright eyes, a thought-
ful brow, and something unusual and arresting in appearance
and expression. She was most precise and punctual in all her
habits, visiting daily her gardens, glasshouses and farm, her
aviary of rare birds, managing personally every department of
her property, and never resting until perfectly satisfied with
what she saw. No detail, however small, escaped her notice.
Her knowledge, indeed, covered a wide ground, for she was
well acquainted with the art, literature and history of many
countries. She was most interested in animal life, loving her
dogs devotedly. Original in mind and speech, she had a great
sense of humour, and could express herself both easily and
with point in three languages '.

I first met her in 1913 and found that at the age of 67 she
was a sparkling conversationalist and most entertaining, but
she had one idiosyncracy which was rather unnerving. Whenever she said something amusing, as often happened, and one
laughed, she would round on one, and ask with machine-gun
speed ' Why do you laugh? '. Her health, since the first attack

Detail of a harp in Miss
Alice's collection: French
workmanship of the late
eighteenth century

of rheumatic fever, had deteriorated and for some years she had been told that it would be unwise for her to spend the winters in England. So she had bought herself a villa at Grasse, in the South of France, where she spent the months from October to April, constructing what I believe was an outstanding garden which went half way up a mountain behind her villa. But Waddesdon was seldom out of her thoughts and a constant flow of instructions, enquiries and exhortations would flow from Grasse to Waddesdon throughout the winter months.

At Waddesdon she is still spoken of in terms of reverence, even awe, and anecdotes continue to be told of her which betray the strange mixture of alarm and yet real affection and pride in which she was held. She had almost impossibly high standards and would tolerate nothing but the best. Indeed, the phrase 'Waddesdon standard' became current in her day, and is still in use as typifying the degree of perfection which can only be achieved by intensive trouble-taking. But her real kindness is also well-remembered, both to individuals and to the neighbourhood as a whole. Her improvements to the amenities of Waddesdon village were countless and included schools, a nursing home and clubs for recreation. The more elegant of the clubs, which was furnished with a library of leather bound classics, was named the Institute and in those hierarchical days was reserved for the estate 'Heads of Department' and tenant farmers only. The other club, possibly jollier if less literate, was for the lesser fry of the village. The 'School Treats' which she continued to provide each year lost none of the glamour they had acquired in her brother's time. Her sense of piety and conservation induced her to take immense trouble to arrange the removal of a crusader's tomb from the now crumbling chapel at Eythrope to the safety of the nave of Waddesdon parish church.

In the Manor itself, one of her first cares must have been to re-adorn the Smoking Room and the long corridor outside it whose contents her brother had bequeathed to the British Museum. Being as passionate a collector as her brother she had already filled three houses—one in Piccadilly, her winter home at Grasse and the Pavilion at Eythrope—with enchanting pictures and furniture, mostly of the eighteenth century. I think she must have welcomed the opportunity given her by the bare walls of the Smoking Room to indulge her collecting instincts once again, and to some extent in a new field. She re-furnished the Smoking Room with many small pictures of the sixteenth and seventeenth centuries, Limoges enamels and Venetian and Bohemian glass. She hung the walls of the corridor outside it with small arms which she found and chose with the

Philippe Egalité, duc d'Orleans, at the age of 2, by François Boucher.

80

help of her friend, Sir Guy Laking, who was in charge of the Armour at Windsor and the Tower.

In the rest of the house she made very few changes, only adding one major picture and some snuff boxes. I believe she wished to change Waddesdon as little as possible and so preserve it intact as a memorial to her brother's taste and knowledge.

If Waddesdon's creation was due to Baron Ferdinand, its state of preservation is most certainly due to his sister. He was once described to me by an old friend who remembered him happily puffing a cigar all over his house, and I have no doubt he allowed the sun to shine in on his guests and light up the carpets, furniture and books he loved so much. Not so Miss Alice. In her day, smoking was most rigourously restricted to the Smoking Room and the continual adjustment of blinds which she enforced prevented all harmful rays of the sun from falling on textiles, marquetry and drawings. She laid down the most stringent rules about who should be allowed to touch china. No female hand was allowed to dust the decorative Sèvres vases in the various sitting-rooms; this was the responsibility of one particularly trusted man only. The Sèvres and Dresden china used in the dining room, however, was washed up by the Housekeeper and the Still-Room Maid, who did it in accordance with Miss Alice's simple but effective standing order: 'When touching china, *always* use two hands and maintain complete silence'. Visitors to Waddesdon to-day sometimes comment on the remarkable state of preservation of its contents which they find singularly unfaded, unbattered and unchipped. When they do so they are, unknowingly, paying a tribute to Miss Alice's constant and unwavering care.

There was only one part of Waddesdon in which, I think, she believed she could better her brother's administration; this was the garden. If the fruit, flowers and vegetables grown at Waddesdon had not proved absolutely perfect, or plentiful, Baron Ferdinand would not, I think, have been averse to making up the supplies he wanted from any convenient outside source. Miss Alice had other views. After her brother's death one of her first problems was to find a head gardener for Waddesdon who would be able to attain her more exacting standards. One highly recommended man after another was first engaged and then despatched as a disappointing failure. Having exhausted all obvious sources of recruitment without success Miss Alice then asked her trusted old French gardener at Grasse for advice. Without hesitation he told her she would not go wrong if she considered the promotion of a young Englishman, G. F. Johnson, who had been working in her mountain garden at Grasse for

Parade shield, probably made by Eliseus Libaertz of Antwerp for François I of France.

81

Hand mirror backed with a
Limoges enamel plaque, by
Jean de Court, depicting the
Rape of Europa: sixteenth
century

Eighteenth century Dutch
dolls' house silver collected
by Miss Alice

the past four years. Miss Alice took this advice, judging that the enterprise and determination already shown by Johnson in his career outweighed the risk of appointing someone aged only 26 to be in charge of the very large garden staff at Waddesdon.

Johnson's career had indeed been unusual. He was the son of a gardener who had done his best to dissuade him from following his own profession. Young Johnson, however, was determined to garden, and learnt his trade from Veitch, the great nurseryman, whose business was, in effect, a horticultural university. Through the friendship of his father with Baron Ferdinand's valet, he then secured a much coveted entry into the Waddesdon gardens. Having passed through all the departments there, he felt the need to learn the German language and asked the Head Gardener at Waddesdon to recommend him to his opposite number in Vienna where Baron Ferdinand's brother had a superb garden which was especially noted for its fruit grown under glass. This request was refused, and no introduction was given. Johnson, however, decided to take a chance; he took himself to Vienna, and was engaged to work in Baron Nathaniel's garden. After four years there he decided to learn French and again without introduction he reached Grasse in the South of France. He happened to present himself at Miss Alice's garden when she herself was there. His arrival caused a little commotion and Miss Alice asked what was happening. She was told that a young Englishman who had worked in the gardens of two of her brothers, in England and in Austria, was applying for a job with her. Not unnaturally, this made Miss Alice look upon him with some interest, and he was engaged on the spot. Not only did she appreciate his initiative in travelling the world, but even his extreme youth seemed to be an advantage; there was every chance that he could be trained up to fit her own sky-high standards.

Not long after Johnson's return to Buckinghamshire Miss Alice pointed out to him how desirable it was that the Head Gardener at Waddesdon should be married, and almost his first commission was to seek out a wife. Fortunately, Johnson had no objection to complying with this order and his admirable choice of spouse immediately met with Miss Alice's approval. He lived to celebrate 62 years in the family's service before dying in 1954 and throughout all those years he grew to perfection, first for Miss Alice and then for my husband, the special strains of flowers, fruit and vegetables she had sought out and collected from all over Europe. To this day I can remember the flavour of a variety of almost black strawberry, called I think 'Waterloo' with which she regaled us in 1913. Sadly, two wars later, this strain has now died out.

The private sitting room at
Waddesdon allotted to Miss
Alice by her brother, which
remained unchanged until
her death

I think Miss Alice considered it her duty to maintain the
reputation for hospitality which had been established by her
brother, so throughout the summer, when she was there, she
continued to run Waddesdon on the same lines, and on the
same scale. Many of his old friends—who were also hers—came
to stay, as well as new ones. Her parties were not so large nor
so numerous as his, and were noticeably less political. But
politicians still came: Sir Willam Harcourt, the Chancellor of the
Exchequer; Lord Rowton, Disraeli's trusted Private Secretary

Lancret. *Scene from the Italian comedy*

and biographer; and Mr. Winston Churchill again—no longer a youth with political aspirations, but now the Member for Oldham and with the charge at Omdurman and his escape from the Boers behind him. As the years went by she acquired many new friends while remaining faithful to the old: among her later acquaintances was Lord Kitchener who shared her own interest in the collecting of works of art.

There is no doubt that the friendship of the Royal Family for Baron Ferdinand also extended to his sister. During Queen Victoria's last years she too had sought the sun in winter, and when staying at the Grand Hotel in Grasse was a frequent visitor at Miss Alice's 'Villa Victoria'—so named by permission. Holidays in the South of France were taken rather differently in those days. In the evenings, the Queen would ask Miss Alice to come and sit with her, and on one occasion also invited Lady Battersea who was staying with Miss Alice. In her 'Reminiscences' Lady Battersea records: 'One evening the Queen sent for my cousin and myself. We found Her Majesty sitting in a

85

Venetian glass goblet

small room at the hotel, listening whilst at work, to Princess Beatrice who was playing duets on the piano with the Queen's maid-of-honour, Marie Adeane, H.M. beating time with her crochet hook'. Lady Battersea also noted that the Queen, when speaking of her privately, invariably referred to Miss Alice as 'The All-Powerful', and was astonished at her energy and capability, especially in the continual enlargement of her mountain garden which the Queen often traversed in her donkey-chair.

In the new reign Queen Alexandra was a guest at Waddesdon as was King Edward who came again to plant a tree in memory of his old friend, Baron Ferdinand. To the end of her days, Miss Alice was invariably invited to the children's garden-parties at Marlborough House; evidently, her hosts there knew of her liking for children who cannot have found her the form-idable figure which Waddesdon legend has sometimes made her out to be.

The last big party she gave at Waddesdon, in 1913, was a dinner for all the officers of the Bucks Yeomanry. This was to celebrate the cessation of a running battle Miss Alice had fought with the British Army over the Yeomanry's temerity in riding over growing crops when on manoeuvres in the park at Waddesdon. So stoutly had this war been waged by both con-testants that I understand it took the combined efforts of two Field-Marshals, the Duke of Connaught and Lord Kitchener, to settle the terms of peace. Typically, Miss Alice ensured that this dinner, to mark the end of hostilities, should be one of the most magnificent she had ever given.

In 1914 the real war started and the saddening changes it brought to the whole country also, of course, affected Waddes-don. Unmarried and childless, Miss Alice nevertheless worried greatly about the fate of her relations, all over Europe. She was particularly saddened by the death in action in Palestine of her English cousin, Evelyn, who she had hoped would succeed her at Waddesdon. No one was more jingo than Miss Alice, but she had the political foresight to gauge correctly the lasting con-sequences of a world war. But at the age of 68 there was little that she, personally, could do to further an Allied victory but to see that potatoes were grown in beds once filled with tea-roses and heliotrope, and arrange for the once immaculately kept lawns to grow much needed hay. Her chief worry, I believe, was to provide enough employment for the young wives of her erstwhile household, stablemen and farmers who were away fighting, and to find what means she could to com-fort those whose husbands and sons would never return. During the winters Bournemouth became her refuge instead of Grasse, to which she only returned in 1919. For some years her health had deteriorated and in May 1922, while she was on her way back from Grasse to Waddesdon she died in a Paris hotel. From August 1915 until Miss Alice died, there are no signatures in the Waddesdon visitors' book.

James de Rothschild
1922-1957

I UNDERSTAND that in the last years of her life Miss Alice, realistic as always, refused to make any long term plans for the garden or the farms. Those in charge were repeatedly told 'that is for my heirs to decide'. She wanted them to be able to make their own choice of the manner in which the estate should be carried on. As my husband was her heir we appreciated this freedom enormously.

Both Baron Ferdinand and Miss Alice had enjoyed the company of their young nephews and great-nephews who were all often asked to stay at Waddesdon, so for a number of years my husband had known his great-aunt quite well. He and I became engaged to be married one Saturday in January, 1913. On the following day he came again to my parents' house in Carlton Gardens (which has now become the official residence of the Foreign Secretary) and from there we walked to Charing Cross Post Office which then, as now, is open for business at all hours of every day including Sundays. My fiancé said he was going to send telegrams to all his many relatives, announcing our engagement, and that if I watched him doing so he would give me a first lesson in who was who in his complicated family. We reached the Post Office and he began to write out the telegrams, giving me a short description of each intended recipient as he did so. When he came to the telegram to Miss Alice he said ' This one is important—and I bet it never gets there!' and explained to me that of all his family Miss Alice would be the only one to mind if she first read of our engagement in the newspapers. He had no reason whatever to think this telegram to Miss Alice would miscarry, but mysteriously, his light-hearted prophecy proved correct. Of all the telegrams sent that day the one to Miss Alice, through some unknown postal mishap, alone failed to arrive.

Although she felt the omission at the time, her vexation was short-lived and she was kind enough to ask us to Waddesdon soon after our marriage. In her remaining years I began to feel that I knew her quite well; I did not see her often, as the

James de Rothschild
(1878–1957)

first war followed almost immediately, and after 1916 she lived the secluded life of an invalid, but throughout all the period we were in touch by letter. Perhaps I felt I knew her better than I did, for I also heard much about her from her sister, Mathilde— my husband's grandmother—and also from my mother-in-law, her contemporary, who had been a close friend of her youth. But never, at any time, did it occur to me, any more than it did to my husband, that Waddesdon might, one day, be our home.

My husband, who was known to everyone as Jimmy, was born and brought up in Paris. He was a grandson of the founder of the French branch of the family. He was always delicate as a child, but at the age of three spoke French, English and German with the accent of a native in each tongue. He too, followed the family tradition in his youth, by making a collection of Greek and Roman coins, but these, like his stamp album, were put away with maturity. He ended his French schooldays—made nightmarish by the anti-semitism engendered by the Dreyfus affair—by being the head of his *Lycée*, Louis le Grand, and in an examination, the *Concours Général* which in those days extended to the whole of France, he again emerged top, with the title of '*caçique*'. When he was eighteen he was sent to Cambridge, where for three years his thoughts were concentrated not on works of art, nor on his books, but rather on hunting and steeple-chasing. He longed to remain at Cambridge for a fourth year, but his father agreed that he should do so only if he won a scholastic prize. With the remarkable concentration of which he was always capable, he switched his attention, for a few months, to intensive study and secured the Harkness Prize with his essay 'Shakespeare and his Day' which was subsequently published. After this year of grace he was sent to Hamburg to learn the rudiments of banking, but contrived, by enduring long night journeys, to spend his occasional free days hunting or steeple chasing in England. Following serious concussion he sustained through a fall at Cottenham, he emigrated under an assumed name to Australia, hoping to avoid entering the Paris branch of the family bank. For eighteen months he successfully eluded his family's attempts to find him and earned his living in various ways, starting as a book-maker's runner on the Melbourne race-course and ending as a cattle-hand on a northern ranch. Much to his annoyance, but to his parents' great relief, his whereabouts were traced by his English cousin Alfred, who prided himself on his world-wide connections. Thanks to this intervention and to his own feelings of remorse at causing his family so much anxiety, he met his parents in Ceylon and returned to France with them. His father thought perhaps a world tour with one of his Cambridge friends, Vere Ponsonby, might

90

James de Rothschild (2nd from right) in Palestine in 1918. On the left, Dr. Chaim Weizmann: 2nd from left, The Hon. William Ormsby Gore

soften the transition from roughing it in Australia to life in a Paris bank. This intuitive idea proved a good one; the two young men went literally round the world: Canada, the United States, China and India were included in their itinerary. In China he had the astonishing experience of dining with the famous Empress Dowager, an occasion made all the better for Jimmy by his always adventurous taste in food. He ate all the local delicacies, including 100-year old eggs, with relish. Vere Ponsonby was far from sharing his pleasure in this respect: I sympathise with him as I also much prefer roast chicken and a normal boiled hen's egg to any other form of food. Their visit to India coincided with Lord Curzon's Durbar—another flamboyant and memorable occasion. But the Paris bank awaited him, and in this he worked hard and took a prominent part until the 1914 war started.

His experiences in the war were varied: he started as a *poilu* in the French army and was seconded to the British army with the rank of '*Interprète Stagiaire*'. Many of Jimmy's peace-time friends were on the staff of the British 3rd Corps, to which he was attached and so he was invited to join the mess of the Corps' C.O., General Pulteney. Here the red trousers of Jimmy's *poilu* uniform and his non-commissioned rank caused some hilarity, although he was ultimately taken seriously enough to be awarded the D.C.M. In 1915 he was badly injured near Bailleul when a large lorry in which he was travelling overturned, pinning him beneath it. Fortunately a British platoon came by, led by an officer who stopped to enquire

91

The author's father and
mother, Mr and Mrs Eugéne
Pinto

what had happened. An explanation was given with the
comment that the figure whose head, buried in the mud, was
just protruding from the side of the lorry, was that of a dead
man. The officer stirred the mud with his boot, thus revealing
the face of the body, and then exclaimed 'My God! It's Jimmy
Rothschild! Dig him up'. It still took some while for this order
to be carried out, and during that time Jimmy could hear,
but not see, other passers-by on that shell-torn road. He
recognised two English voices as belonging to acquaintances
of his peace-time days. The first voice—that of a General—
asked:

'Is there anyone under there?'

'Yes' replied the General's A.D.C.

'Do you know who it is?'

'Yes, Jimmy Rothschild'

'Is he dead?' asked the General

'Not yet' came the reply.

Jimmy said that the cheerful tone in which this 'Not yet'
was pronounced always made him feel slightly less than friend-

Baron and Baroness Edmond
de Rothschild by Bakst

ly whenever he met the A.D.C. in after years.

He had received multiple injuries, including a broken pelvis, and was despatched to Paris in great pain. Within a few months he tried to resume his interpreter's duties with the 3rd Corps, but his health had been shattered and he was forced to retreat to a spell in the Ministry of Munitions in London. However, his health eventually improved sufficiently for him to return to active service and he spent nearly all 1918 in Palestine where, among his other duties, he raised a Jewish Battalion for service under Allenby. Three of his recruits were named Ben-Gurion, Ben-Zvi and Sprinzak: I don't know how useful they were as infantrymen but more than 30 years later the first became the Prime Minister, the second the President and the third the Speaker of the Parliament of the State of Israel.

This was Jimmy's first visit to Palestine and while he was there he was able to see for himself the colonies which his father had founded, of which he had heard so much. As long ago as 1882 his father, moved by the plight of Russian Jews at the height of the pogroms, had begun his colonisation work in Palestine. By 1918, some of the innumerable difficulties of establishing preponderantly intellectual Jews in an uncultivated desert, or in malarial swamps infested by mosquitoes, had been overcome. Jimmy was captivated by the courage, persistence and ingenuity which had created the existing settlements, with their orchards, oranges, grape-fruit and vines in the midst of a desert landscape and vowed then to do all he could to help his father continue his work, and to further the Zionist cause, which he saw as the one hope of his tortured co-religionists in Eastern Europe.

After the war he had the misfortune to lose an eye while playing golf at Deauville and this proved a lasting handicap: at the end of his life he was almost blind.

In 1919 he applied for British naturalisation, some three years before we were overwhelmed by our totally unexpected inheritance of Waddesdon. I say 'overwhelmed' in no sense of ingratitude, but as our friend, Lord d'Abernon said, when he heard of our good fortune, 'Waddesdon is not an inheritance, it is a career'.

In 1922 I had reached the mature age of 27 and had been a married woman for nine years. In childhood I had had a wonderfully care-free existence: no boarding-school; no exams; a bi-lingual father who always spoke French to me, but who did not, alas, endow me with his adventurous spirit; and a mother who was as enchantingly pretty as she was angelic in character. They made sure that I learnt the rudiments of golf, croquet, lawn tennis, bridge, bézique, riding and waltzing, but

I never had any experience whatever of country life. All our holidays were spent in a small house in Brighton. When Jimmy asked me to marry him I had only just been promoted by my parents to dine with them at 7.45 followed immediately by bed.

Quite apart from emotional feelings, the experiences of the few weeks of our engagement can never be forgotten. The failure of the telegram to reach Miss Alice was not the only complication to arise. Jimmy had telephoned our news to his parents in Paris who had no inkling of his budding romance. The line was not clear and in any case the name of Dorothy Pinto conveyed nothing to them. Their anxiety was great and they telephoned to their cousin Alfred in London, hoping to get more detailed information. Unfortunately his accuracy for once failed him and he reported that Jimmy was engaged to a most charming and beautiful actress, Miss Dorothy Minto, who was a star of the musical comedy stage.

The effect on my future in-laws was devastating; their views on mixed religious marriages were rigid and they had thought they were shared by their eldest child. Mercifully, later and more accurate information freed them from anxiety and within four days my father, mother, Jimmy and I set off to see them.

My total lack of imagination fortunately spared me any anticipation of the ordeals which lay before us. Straight from the Gare du Nord Jimmy and I were conveyed in his family's electric motor to his paternal home in the Faubourg St. Honoré, next door to the British Embassy. To Jimmy's embarrassment, the household took the view that our arrival was a momentous occasion; the lodge gates were flung open and we drove into a brilliantly illuminated courtyard and entered the house by the imposing front door, instead of by the customary cosy little side-door which I used ever after.

We were received by my prospective in-laws on the first floor, to the accompaniment of the shrill barking of a dachshund and a Skye terrier, both quite out of control. Fortunately, Jimmy's parents' smiles of welcome obliterated the mounting terror of the dogs as they swirled round my legs.

There followed, that evening, a small dinner party—not at the Faubourg's usual hour of 8.30, but at 7.45, to suit my father who always maintained that 7.46 was too late to begin eating. Sir Frank Bertie, the British Ambassador, was the only other guest, but after dinner all members of the Rothschild family in Paris were invited to come and have a look at the prospective bride—an interesting ordeal for me.

My father had two sisters and a brother living in Paris, and they all wished to give dinner parties for us. It was most kind,

Above Caricature of Mr. & Mrs. James de Rothschild by Sem

Opposite James and Dorothy de Rothschild at Wisbech in the 1929 election

but the existing French custom enjoined that engaged couples, after dinner, should be ushered into a different room from the other guests, and should stay there throughout the evening, with the door left wide open to ensure propriety. The element of the ridiculous in this situation made it hard for us to accept it gracefully.

Trousseau hunting filled the days, and at the end of an exhausting week we were invited to stay with Jimmy's cousins at Ferrières, a huge house in the country modelled on Mentmore. There a large house-party was invited to meet us. Unfortunately, my mother was unaware that in France the principal guest was expected to give the signal for the end of the evening and bed—she was more accustomed to the English habit of depending on the hostess for this relief. Far, far too late, a solution to this impasse was found and, dropping with fatigue, we thankfully got upstairs. On our return to England I then faced a further round of introductions to Jimmy's huge family here. This included a visit to Lord Rosebery, to whose charm I fell an instant victim, but whose personality was distinctly alarming until one got accustomed to his brilliant banter.

Looking back on those hectic days before our wedding on February 25th, it is difficult to realise that most of those hurried introductions led ultimately to many friendships which have been one of the delights of my life.

After our honeymoon spent hunting at Pau and touring Spain we settled down—if that is the word—to a pattern of life which consisted of continuous travel. Just before we married, Jimmy had bought a house in London, in Park Street, and in Paris we lived in his bachelor flat in the Champs Elysées. As he was still a member of the French branch of the family bank, our days were divided between his work in Paris, and his racing in England. We also went further afield. I was taken to stay with his wonderful grandmother, Baroness Willy, the sister of Baron Ferdinand and Miss Alice, who lived in Frankfort. Our first visit covered the period when she and I both had birthdays in March, she became 81 while I achieved 18. She was not only brilliant intellectually, but also endowed with that rare quality of understanding that made her the confidante of all the members of her family. She shared the linguistic talents of her brother and sister and, in addition, was an accomplished musician—a pupil of Chopin, and a composer herself. At Waddesdon there is a complete collection of the music she wrote, mostly songs which were sung by such famous artists as Mme. Patti. When I knew her she was the widow of the most religious member of the Rothschild family and although she survived her husband by twenty-three years,

'The Pink Boy'—
Gainsborough's portrait of
Master Nicholls.

96

she never forsook the exacting Orthodox life to which he had accustomed her. We spent Passover with her in 1913, with Jimmy officiating as closely as he could in the tradition of his grandfather. As I was the youngest person present it fell to my lot to ask the ritual questions in Hebrew—another experience I shall never forget. Even when we were in London, the change from childhood's regular routine to the whirl of married life could not have been greater. I found myself a member of a huge new family, with a brilliant husband who had many friends in all walks of life, particularly in the to me unknown worlds of politics and racing.

But no sooner had I become used to this existence than the 1914 war came. I found myself, bereft of the company and guidance of my husband who, when leaving to join the French army on August 1st, insisted that I should remain in England. At least this meant that my parents would not be bereft of both their children during those horrible times and I was able to share with them the anxiety for my brother who had joined the Coldstream. To our joy he did manage to emerge alive in 1918, although not entirely unscathed and with an M.C.

In London, in 1915, I found much friendship in the world of Liberal politics and, having made the acquaintance of Dr. Weizmann, I was also introduced to the hopes which I shared and still share of a Zionist future for Palestine in which my father-in-law was primarily interested. I became the post office which transmitted the views and news of Dr. Weizmann to Baron Edmond and vice versa.

When Jimmy returned to England and worked in the Ministry of Munitions while his injuries were healing, we were together again until he was well enough to join the army once more, and went off to Palestine. This time he agreed that I might go to France where I remained until the end of 1918—a strange experience, but one which enabled me really to get to know my parents-in-law, a memory I shall always cherish.

It was my hope when peace came and Jimmy returned to England, we should lead a more normal existence at last. But our first days were disrupted by the worry and pain occasioned by Jimmy's loss of his eye, and then in 1921 we started to travel again. First we went to the United States and to Canada on behalf of the Zionist cause, and then, after hardly a pause, we went to Palestine. Here we had the unusual experience of being the guests of the High Commissioner, Sir Herbert Samuel, simultaneously with Mr. and Mrs. Winston Churchill and the Emir Abdullah, while the Emirate of Jordan was being planned.

I have only given this account of my early days in order to show that although by 1922 they had had a certain variety,

Gainsborough's portrait of Lady Sheffield.

97

nothing in my upbringing or experience had prepared me for life in the English countryside or, indeed, at Waddesdon.

It was with feelings of apprehension that we faced this fateful new future which had so suddenly opened before us. Obviously, we had to take the plunge and visit Waddesdon at the earliest opportunity, but we could not rid ourselves of the feeling of being interlopers taking over what had been a closely guarded preserve. Jimmy felt strongly that he wished to avoid any impression that might be given to Miss Alice's mourning household of a brash new heir arriving with a swagger, and decided that it would be more modest if we travelled from London by train. As our own motor met us at Aylesbury station to drive us the six miles to Waddesdon I never quite understood the point of this manoeuvre, although I shared the feelings which prompted it.

One of the more alarming consequences of our inheritance was the prospect of finding myself in charge of a large household staff. But Miss Alice had been a shrewd judge of character and she could never have chosen more wisely than in Mrs. Boxall, her housekeeper, who received us on our arrival. White-haired, but with a young pink and white complexion, she had an encyclopaedic knowledge of all the arts of conservation on which Miss Alice had so much insisted. In the following months it was she who told me of Miss Alice's rules for handling china, and it was she who explained how textiles should be treated in a perfectly run house. I was let into the secrets of the great cupboards in the North and South Linen Rooms and was shown the enchantingly pretty patterned linen covers which Miss Alice had had made for every chair in the house. In her philosophy, as in Mrs. Boxall's, tapestry and silk upholstery should only be allowed to be visible when there were guests in the house.

To my great relief I found the various heads of department would relieve me of the responsibilities of recruitment. It was only in the dire event of one of the 'heads' themselves leaving that we would be expected to find and engage their successor.

Mrs. Boxall reigned supreme over all the women in the house, as did the Steward over the male staff. The living quarters of the men were as far removed as possible from that of their female colleagues. Indeed, there was no direct route from the top floors of the batchelors' wing, in which the men lived, to the main part of the house. Nevertheless, I came to understand that these stringent precautionary measures were not entirely successful, and that an ingenious if unorthodox means had been evolved of at least gaining the housemaids' sitting-room.

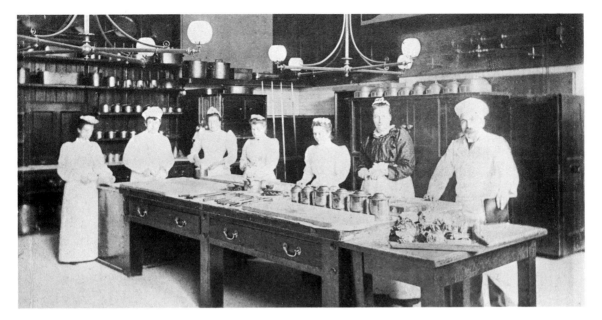

The kitchen staff at
Waddesdon, c. 1910

The third department in the house, beyond the control of either the Steward or the Housekeeper, was the kitchen. Here a French Chef held undisputed sway, even over the Italian Pastry Cook who operated in a separate room. One of the walls of the main kitchen was entirely taken up by great coal-fired ranges and ovens. Another longer wall was covered in shelves which bore row upon row of shining copper pans. Variously shaped for every culinary purpose, and in every size, each of these bore a monogram—F. R. on the older ones, and A. R. on the more modern.

In these gleaming surroundings the Chef was aided by five assistants, the more senior of whom wore a coloured blouse; all the others were clothed in white from head to toe. Not only were the Chef and all his assistants talented and dexterous but, it seemed to me, they also appeared to be possessed of immense physical strength. Some of the coppers needed two people to carry them, even when they were empty, and it must have required a Hercules to close or open some of the great oven doors. Of all the changes in daily living which have come about in my life-time I think the greatest may be in the preparation and cooking of food. When I compare what was done in the Waddesdon kitchen when I first knew it with the simplicity of heating up a pre-cooked meal from a freezer, it hardly seems possible that both methods are equally successful in warding off hunger—if not of satisfying taste. The only thing which seems to have remained constant is the preoccupation about getting fat.

The still-room, as in other houses where one existed, did

not come under the Chef, but was part of the Housekeeper's kingdom. Although both the kitchen and the still-room produced food, their work was divided by an exact, well-understood, but seemingly inexplicable line of demarcation. Many years later, I asked a beloved ex-still-room maid to remind me of the work of her department. She gave me a mouth-watering description of the scones, jams and tisanes which had been made in the still-room and ended by saying 'And, of course, we washed and prepared the parsley for the sandwiches—but naturally, we did not make the sandwiches themselves; that was kitchen work'.

By the end of 1922, the Pastry Cook had departed, and by what would now be called 'natural wastage' the numbers in each department were diminished, but the internal structure and discipline of the house remained.

Out of doors, neither Baron Ferdinand nor Miss Alice had thought it necessary to employ an Agent—a superior being who would have been in ultimate charge of everything, both in the house and in the surrounding estate. I think they had preferred to deal more directly themselves with the chiefs of all the separate entities. These included not only the Home Farms, the tenant farms, the garden and the stables but also the Forestry department, which tended the woodlands and the fences, and the Works staff which maintained the farm buildings and the many cottages and village houses in which the employees of the estate lived.

Relations with the tenant farmers were conducted by Mr. Sims, who had once been in charge of the tree-planting in the Baron's day, and who had since been promoted to Farm Bailiff. As such he was, apparently, responsible for supplying us with a list of the type of poultry each employee would prefer as a gift at Christmas time. We were somewhat startled by our first experience of this list; presented without a heading or any explanation, its first line read: 'Myself—a Goose'.

In those days, before the complexities of insurance contributions and V.A.T. had even been thought of, there had, it seems, been no need for an estate accountant. We found that everyone on the estate, both indoor and outdoor, was paid by the family lawyer who, once a fortnight, drove the six miles from Aylesbury—at first in a horse fly but latterly in a more modern conveyance—bearing with him a Gladstone bag stuffed with the necessary money.

Overwhelmed as we were by our new surroundings, our instinctive wish was to make as few alterations as possible. But one or two changes in the house had to be tackled immediately. Baron Ferdinand, ever an enterprising man, had

Part of the greenhouse range at Waddesdon

been one of the first in the country to convert the lighting in his house from gas to electricity. He did this in the days when, if you wanted such a new-fangled invention, you had to make the electricity yourself. His installation, dependent on a power house secreted in a grove of chestnuts by the back door, was plainly insufficient to deal with more modern needs and appliances.

We decided to re-wire the whole house to cope with the stronger supply we hoped to introduce and then found, to our intense surprise, that the drainage was also suspect. Seemingly Waddesdon's drains had been installed without the meticulous care which had been lavished on all the other components of the building. The suspicion that we have today that the Prince Consort's early death from typhoid was due to defective drainage at Windsor Castle was a theory unknown to Baron Ferdinand or Miss Alice and to many of their contemporaries: if they had had an inkling of it, I can well imagine the speed with which they would have taken steps to improve the drainage in their own houses. As it was, the whole system had to be renewed, and while this was being done we took the opportunity to install one or two more bathrooms. There were already some in the house, as both Baron Ferdinand and Miss Alice had catered for the more modern notions of some of their guests, but to the end of her days Miss Alice, like some others of her age, had preferred a hip bath.

In the event, we also found we were obliged to make considerable changes in the garden, principally in the glass-houses, which must have been as extensive as any in the country. It was in their management, I believe, that Miss Alice

101

had had such difficulty in finding a head-gardnener competent to meet her needs. The houses were divided into four sections—first for display *in situ*, in what was known as the 'Top Glass' which, in turn was fed by the growing houses which also produced the flowers used for indoor decoration as well as the many gifts of malmaison carnations, orchids and other delights with which visitors to Waddesdon were often sent home. Thirdly, there was the colossal Fruit Range, and finally the heated frames in which were grown the early vegetables before the outdoor varieties were ready.

Mr. Johnson, whose career I have already mentioned, was responsible for all this as well, of course, for the herbaceous borders, the rose garden, the rock garden and the 'bedding out' round the house which, as contemporary photographs show, was of unbelievable elaboration. During his many years at Waddesdon Mr. Johnson managed to hand on at least some of his almost unique knowledge to whole new generations of gardeners, but learning from him was certainly no sinecure. I heard later from some of those who had done so that whenever, in the course of one's work, one happened to come within his view, it was essential not to be seen with a cigarette in one's mouth and—if one was to escape his wrath—also to be seen moving at the double: it was not only speed, but also the most

Cyclamen grown for market in glasshouses previously devoted to semi-tropical plants

Daffodil Valley: Chestnuts
and Sycamore on the left:
Wellingtonia on the right

minute attention to every detail that he demanded from those who worked under him.

We came to the sad conclusion that the beautiful Alamandas, Bougainvillia and Gloriosa Rothschildiana which ramped up the central sections of the 'Top Glass' would have to be scrapped and that the exotic species in many of the other houses must also go. Their place was taken by commercial cyclamen grown on a vast scale; they, too, had their beauty especially when massed together in great sheets of colour when awaiting the lorries to take them to Covent Garden. One exception was made in the general holocaust of plants which required great heat to thrive; these were the anthuriums which continued to be preserved for a number of years. Greatly daring, we decided to exhibit the anthuriums at one of the Royal Horticultural Society's shows at Vincent Square, where they were awarded a Gold Medal. That accolade only underlined the probable quality of all the other exotic plants we had so reluctantly abolished. But the huge fairyland of semi-tropical colour so enthusiastically created by our predecessors had ceased, in the 1920's, to be a viable project for any private garden to harbour. In the Fruit Range Miss Alice's carefully selected figs, peaches, nectarines and grapes continued to flourish. I am thankful to say that in

103

newer and much more modest quarters a few of their descendants are still alive to-day.

The only change we made in the garden at Waddesdon which might be called an improvement was to enable the flowering season to start in the early spring. Miss Alice had always been obliged to miss this enchanting moment in England, owing to her rigid time-table. Our most notable success was the planting of what is now rightly called Daffodil Valley, just below the Aviary, which is one of the out-door delights to greet our visitors at Easter time.

Never can any man have had less incentive, or need, than Jimmy to make a personal collection of works of art. Quite apart from the unexpected inheritance of Waddesdon, he would, in the nature of things, one day inherit a share of his father's possessions. Baron Edmond was one of the most notable collectors of his time, and indeed some of the loveliest

Limoges panel attributed to Jean de Court. *Juno and the Three Furies*. Second half of the sixteenth century

Limoges ewer

George Belcher's cartoon of
James de Rothschild racing

The Ascot Gold Cup of
1909

Opposite James de Rothschild
leading in *Bomba*, the
winner of the Gold Cup at
odds of 33–1

furniture, drawings, manuscripts, Limoges enamels and Renaissance jewels which are now at Waddesdon, as well as paintings by Watteau and Rubens, were bequeathed to Jimmy by his father. Born in 1845, the youngest son of a youngest son, Baron Edmond had been only 23 years old when he inherited from his father, the first Baron James, many outstanding works of art, and throughout the course of a long life he had never ceased to add to them. He was only nine years old when he first began to gather together the astonishing number of engravings which, on his death at the age of 89, he left to the Louvre. He studied these engravings with passion, and knew them so well that even when he was almost completely blind, he could describe the detail of any one of the thousands he owned, and the differences in the 'states' of the same composition. He maintained that these engravings were the source of much of his knowledge of his other works of art, and whenever something in his house was to be constructed, from a cornice or a moulding, to a doorway or a frame, he used his engravings as an infallible reference and pattern.

It is not difficult to understand, therefore, why most of Jimmy's personal additions to Waddesdon were outside the house. His improvements on the estate were varied; they included a number of modern cottages and additional holes to the 9-hole golf course Miss Alice had laid out in the park. Jimmy continued to enjoy playing himself despite the loss of his eye on the Deauville links. The Waddesdon course was helpful during a house-party but was mainly used by players from the immediate locality.

Jimmy also built a stud farm to house his brood mares. This was set on a hill with sweeping views of the Vale of Aylesbury from its surrounding paddocks. Racing had been one of his principal delights from boyhood and lasted all his life. He won two Gold Cups—one at Ascot, and one its war-time equivalent run at Newmarket in 1917—as well as many other good races, including the French Grand Prix and two Cambridgeshires, but except for one victory in the One Thousand Guineas, the Classics eluded him. The Derby winner, Gainsborough, was one of the most famous stallions in that era and one of the jokes I remember was that if my husband had had rather fewer Gainsboroughs on the walls of his house, and rather more in his Stud, he might have done better. But the few major successes he had on the Turf over a long period were no gauge of the amount of pleasure he derived from racing. He brought off one, I think, unprecedented coup, which I remember vividly. He won the Jockey Club Stakes—a distance race—and the Cambridgeshire—a much shorter one—with the same horse,

106

Milenko, in 1921, well within a period of two months. It was one of his more unlikely ideas to succeed; the general experience being that it is in any case difficult to train a horse within a short time to run first a short and then a long distance course, but to do it in reverse order was next to impossible.

Perhaps because of his appearance and personality even his most minor exploits on the race-course always appeared to be newsworthy. He bought a mare called Tishy from Sir Abe Bailey which had the doubtful fame of having crossed her legs when running as the favourite in the Cesarewitch. Jimmy had faith in her, however, and she subsequently won a small race for him—not a feat to make race-course history—but the following day almost every newspaper contained a cartoon of some sort celebrating Jimmy and Tishy's mini-victory.

One of his earliest failures was with a horse of his which he fancied tremendously, named Snow Leopard. The day following the race in which all Jimmy's hopes had been misplaced on him, he was re-named Slow Leopard, much to the amusement of the race-going public.

He always said that the first race he had ever witnessed had been his undoing; this was the Epsom Derby of 1898, when the winner, Mr. Larnach's Jeddah, priced at 100 to 1, had been selected by Jimmy for his very first wager. From that day on his support was always attracted by an outsider. A caustic friend said that many people were known to back outsiders, but Jimmy alone appeared to attempt to breed from them.

Always delighting in the unlikely and unorthodox and loving any upset of the accepted norm in his recreations, he was nevertheless one whose judgment and wisdom were indisputable in the more serious matters of life.

Between 1922 and 1939 we gradually accustomed ourselves to the joys and problems involved in making our home at Waddesdon. Among the joys was that of finding ourselves in the proximity of other family houses. I think the fact that Tring, Aston Clinton, Ascott, Mentmore and Halton were all within riding distance from Waddesdon may well have influenced Baron Ferdinand in his selection of the land.

In our day, Halton had already been sold to the Air Ministry, but all the other houses were still lived in by cousins, and could be reached by no more than half an hour's drive. We only once went to Aston Clinton, to see Lady Battersea, one of Sir Anthony de Rothschild's two daughters. As both she and her sister, Annie Yorke, had country houses of their own, and were only able to spend one month a year together in their father's old home, Aston Clinton was sold soon after we came to

Waddesdon. The house was for a time a preparatory school, and after various other transmutations, it was finally destroyed by fire. But its gloriously wooded park has survived and is now a centre for youth activities and sport, in the care of the Bucks County Council.

Tring Park remained the home of Lady Rothschild, her son, the second Lord Rothschild and her daughter-in-law Mrs. Charles Rothschild, two of whose brood of four children have gained distinction—Dr. Miriam Rothschild in the entomological world, and her scientist brother, Lord Rothschild of Think Tank fame. Tring Museum, with its great collection of butter-flies, moths, fleas and other insect curiosities, which was founded by the second Lord Rothschild, still flourishes as a section of the British Museum, but the house itself has become a ballet school. In our day, however, the links between Tring and Waddesdon were very close and enjoyable. The same can be said of Mentmore and Ascott. In 1922, the ex-Prime Minister Rosebery, the widowed husband of Hannah de Rothschild, still lived at Mentmore. In 1923 he gave it to his son, Harry, Lord Dalmeny and following this transfer it became a centre of hunting activity. Its new owner was Master of the Whaddon Chase and locally the many female followers of this popular hunt became known as ' The Harriers '. Lord Rosebery's famous Crafton Stud continued its triumphant influence on the breed-ing of race-horses and I need hardly say it was the subject of intensely interested conversation between the owners of Ment-more and Waddesdon.

Mentmore now stands empty, but Ascott still remains, hav-ing been given, like Waddesdon, to the National Trust. In 1922 it was Mrs. Leopold de Rothschild who lived there with her son Anthony, and many an hour we spent there enjoying their out-standing hospitality. Anthony's son, Evelyn and his wife and family now live there.

After the modernisation of the electricity and the drains we made very few changes in the house at Waddesdon. The main exception was in Miss Alice's private sitting-room on the first floor. It was undeniably a most lovely room, literally crammed, in the Victorian manner, with beautiful furniture, china, pastels and drawings. Its Savonnerie carpet, on which it would have been unthinkable to tread with muddy shoes, had been made in the seventeenth century for the *Grande Galerie* of the Louvre, and was hardly a surface on which one could chuck untidy books and newspapers. But we needed somewhere in which we could tackle the affairs of daily life without being inhibited by the beauty or fragility of our surroundings. So this room was completely emptied; bookcases were put all round the walls;

a plain carpet was laid on the floor and comfortable leather chairs and sofas installed. Emptied of its silks and drawings there was no need in this room to keep a constant and watchful eye on the position of sun-blinds which were here, in fact, abolished. For us it became a blissful snuggery.

The other unchanged rooms in the house were by no means unwelcoming or unused. Waddesdon gave us, as much as to our predecessors, the opportunity to be hospitable. As in earlier days, many of those who now came to stay were politicians, but the House of Commons had changed very much since the 1880's and no comparison can be made between the importance and effectiveness of any meeting of our guests and of those invited by Baron Ferdinand some fifty years earlier. He had been an influential member of the governing Liberal party, whereas Jimmy, also a life-long Liberal, found himself an adherent of a party in opposition which, after a flicker of revival in 1929, steadily declined in numbers and power from that date onwards. For this reason, if for no other, I do not think that in our time the confabulations of leading politicians at Waddesdon can have led to spectacular results on the political life of the country.

In my recollection, I like to think our friends, including even such dominant personalities as Mr. Asquith and Mr. Churchill, regarded Waddesdon as a place where they could relax from their labours and indulge in such pastimes as golf, bézique, bridge and Mah-jong—the most popular games at that time. Any political discussion was largely confined to the period at the end of dinner when, in the English fashion, the ladies retired from the dining-room and the men remained, unencumbered by femininity, to settle down, maybe, to serious talk. However useful these masculine exchanges of view may have been to the participants, I chiefly remember them for the unconscionable length of time they seemed to go on.

In our day Waddesdon was once again honoured by a visit from the reigning Sovereign. The attendant difficulties and dilemmas of this occasion have now been transmuted into pleasurable recollection, but every detail remains vividly in my mind. Even so, I cannot hope to rival Baron Ferdinand in giving an account equal to his of the reception of Queen Victoria.

Unlike Baron Ferdinand who had a whole year in which to prepare for his august visitor, we had comparatively little time. The first intimation was conveyed to me at one of the Spring Meetings at Newmarket in 1926 when the Princess Royal told me that Queen Mary would like to visit Waddesdon, and that the moment Her Majesty had in mind was the afternoon of a not far distant Sunday. It so happened that this particular

The East Gallery in Baron Ferdinand's day

The East Gallery in 1978

110

Sunday came just after the Thursday on which a huge Liberal Fête was to be held at Waddesdon and I immediately pictured what Aunt Alice's feelings would have been at the prospect of the Queen seeing Waddesdon marred and besmirched by the inevitable damage and litter left behind by a crowd of some thousands of people. I therefore pleaded for another date, but no other was available.

So we made what arrangements we could for the prospective damage and mess resulting from the Fête to be cleared up quickly and ordered a beautiful cedar sapling in the expectation that Her Majesty would agree to commemorate her presence by planting it in the time honoured way. Her visit was timed for 3 o'clock and was to include tea.

Everything seemed in order; the political Fête duly took place and an army of helpers moved in to try to obliterate its traces.

Late on the Friday evening we were visiting the Stud when a telephone message was brought to us. It came from Buckingham Palace from the King, asking if he could accompany Queen Mary on the Sunday, and could they come to luncheon?

In a flash I realised the difficulty of dealing with this change of plan in the short time left to us and of securing guests and food for a luncheon party in the country at 24 hours' notice. I also became uneasily aware of my ignorance of the conventions which might rule the reception of a reigning monarch in one's own home—was it for him, for instance, to rise and thus signal the end of luncheon, or was this still the duty of the hostess? Thanks to much telephoning, the provision of food and suitable guests was resolved the following morning, but on seeking advice from Peggy Crewe (a mentor on many problems in my life) I found my ideas about tree planting were not hers. It seemed to me a simple matter that King George should now be asked to plant the cedar, rather than Queen Mary. Peggy said that this was out of the question: it was unthinkable that the King should not be invited to plant a tree and it would be exceedingly rude if the Queen was not also asked to do so: two trees must be provided. I protested that only one was available and that however much she knew about Court manners, she was plainly deficient in her grasp of arboriculture: suitable saplings, I pointed out, did *not* grow on bushes. However, she was adamant, and so I sped to the garden to consult Johnson. He was as resourceful as ever, and calmed my agitation by showing me, just next to the spot where it was planned the cedar should go, an old and fairly rare tree of a species which never exceeded four feet in height, even

A chair from a set of mid 18th century French furniture which is covered in Beauvais tapestry.

112

when fully grown. This he thought could well be dug up and then after suitable titivation, could be returned with ceremony to the hole from whence it came, with no-one being any the wiser. I thankfully agreed to this proposal.

Conversation during luncheon was fascinating. The King remembered with the utmost clarity the occasion of his first visit to Waddesdon when, as a very young man in 1889 he had helped to entertain the Shah of Persia. His account of the varied incidents of that memorable party and the character and appearance of all his fellow guests, was enthralling. At the end he somewhat sadly remarked that he and Ralph Nevill were the only survivors of all those who had been at Waddesdon on that occasion.

Happily, it was a very fine day and after luncheon we went out onto the terrace and stood there for a few moments before moving off to the tree planting. Johnson, in order that the King and Queen should see Waddesdon at its best, had conceived the idea that our appearance should be the signal for a distant tap to be turned on which would operate all the jets of the fountain on the South Terrace. These were rarely made to play, and now they failed in their duty. Instead of emitting graceful cascades of glistening drops high into the sky, they produced a sluggish minimum of water accompanied by a series of gurgles and plops of a distressingly suggestive nature. For several minutes we all stood solemnly listening to these gurgitations: then the Queen was the first to dissolve in laughter and thus released the pent-up giggles of everyone else present. The tree-planting and the rest of the visit was conducted in a spirit of hilarity.

My memories of trying to arrange any agreeable house-party at Waddesdon are also vivid and are tinged with anxiety from start to finish. During the initial period of invitation one composed the perfect party which one learnt from experience would so rarely end up as planned. For excellent but varied reasons some guests would begin by accepting and then chucked; others refused for the date on which they were invited but wondered if they could not come on some other day or days, invariably awkward for oneself. And when the party did assemble I understood all too well Baron Ferdinand's anxiety about his guests' plans and wishes. Presumably we knew in advance who preferred talk to bridge and the relative skills of players of card games, but the plans for the following day always depended so much on the weather—who wished to play golf? Who would be cajoled into visiting the garden or the Stud? Or who might be bent on some intellectual excursion

French clock, c. 1750, decorated with Meissen birds and a figure of Harlequin playing the bag-pipes.

to Oxford? Or who might have business at near-by Chequers?
Preparations for all these possibilities were easier if made in
advance.

In recent years the appreciation of the arts seems to have
grown into a popular fancy. A mass of sight-seers gyrates dis-
cerningly round houses 'open to view' and innumerable
societies devoted to various aspects of the arts appear to flourish. But in the hey-day of our time at Waddesdon things were
very different and any interest in works of art seemed to be a
rarity among our guests. Occasionally some of them conscienti-
ously toured the pictures but more often it was the view out
of the window which caught their eye: china, furniture and
carpets were never objects of interest. However, I do remember
very clearly one remarkable morning when Brendan Bracken
and Leslie Hore Belisha sat, intensely absorbed for at least an
hour, each gazing at one of the two big Guardis which hang
at either end of the East Gallery. Solemnly, from time to time,
they exchanged seats, in total silence.

I don't think any of Baron Ferdinand's more discerning
guests visiting Waddesdon in our day would have noticed
much difference in the arrangement of the rooms. The only
major change was floral; instead of palms pervading the house,

114

The two Guardis bought by
Baron Ferdinand in 1877
round which the East
Gallery was constructed

we substituted flowers, or flowering shrubs—a concession to
modern taste.

In my memory the years between 1922 and 1939 form a somewhat blurred jig-saw of trying to fit in too much in too little
time. My husband's health continually troubled him which
made all plans uncertain. As I remember it, we were never
able to spend much consecutive time at Waddesdon, but were
constantly doomed to flit to London where Jimmy had a mass
of committees to attend, mostly concerned with charities and
Palestine, or to Paris to visit his parents, to whom we were
both devoted. These journeys were interspersed with others
to the variety of race-courses at which devotees of the sport
like to be present, whether they have a horse running or not.
At that time, too, social life had revived and we received many
invitations which necessarily implied at least one night away
from Waddesdon.

In any competition for points indicating preference for a
neighbour at a dinner party, Jimmy would have ranked high.
His very real interest in the lives and opinions of everyone he
met stimulated conversation and seemed to draw from his
neighbours a brilliance and expansiveness which made them
feel they were having an unusually good time. He would not,

115

I think, have been awarded similarly high points at the bridge table. As a player of the cards few could surpass him but his insatiable inclination to try to bring off the seemingly impossible was also a feature of his game. So much so, that I remember one disgruntled player declaring that whenever fate gave him Jimmy as a partner, he could never be sure who was on his side and who was not.

In all his accomplishments he tended to be unexpected. He was always assumed to be a compatriot by Frenchmen, Germans and Englishmen to whom he spoke in their mother tongue and in Hebrew, Spanish and Italian he was by no means tongue-tied. In other languages which he knew less well his marvellous ability to imitate the correct cadence and emphasis in the spoken word always made him sound all right, even if his vocabulary was small. Yet, most surprisingly, he was completely tone-deaf musically. On many occasions, particularly later in life, when attending parliamentary constituency affairs, his failure to recognise the National Anthem in a suitable manner gave me many bad moments if I was too far away from him to take remedial action.

In 1928, in the midst of our days of constant movement, there came a deputation from the Liberal Party Committee of the Isle of Ely, asking Jimmy to be their candidate at the next General Election. The sitting member for the Isle was a Tory, but previously, from 1906 until 1917, it had been held in the Liberal interest by Jimmy's cousin and great friend, Neil Primrose, who was killed in action in 1917. Ever since his Cambridge days, Jimmy had nursed an ambition to become a Liberal Member of Parliament, and this opportunity to contest a seat which, in the past, he had enjoyed helping his cousin to win, was a temptation he could not resist. He won the seat in the 1929 General Election and held it until 1945. So a new and very demanding element entered our lives which reduced even more the ration of time we could spend at Waddesdon.

Nevertheless, Waddesdon remained the anchor of our lives and even provided the scene for some of our major political efforts to propagate Liberal doctrines to mass audiences. The first was the giant 'Liberal Fête' already mentioned, held on the cricket ground where there was a pavilion with a flat roof from which Baron Ferdinand used to address his constituents. Our star speaker at this first Fête was Sir John Simon who attracted a large audience; but this was, perhaps naturally, exceeded by the numbers who, at a later date, came to listen to the Party's leader, Mr. Lloyd George, who spoke at another mass rally. Optimistically, we hoped this one might be an historic occasion and were delighted when Sir John Lavery

The author speaking at a political meeting in the Isle of Ely in 1931

117

accepted our invitation to immortalise it in paint. Although we were wrong in our assumption that that afternoon might have a bearing on the political situation of the day, I am glad that Sir John Lavery's picture of the platform party still hangs at Waddesdon.

Jimmy was an assiduous Member of Parliament and spoke on a variety of subjects—both on those which were of particular interest to his East Anglian constituents, and on topics of international concern. I shall always regret that one day in 1944 I was kept in Aylesbury by my war-time employment and so could not be in the House when he rose to make an impromptu intervention in which he thanked the British people and Government for their treatment of the German Jewish refugees from Hitler who had managed to reach this country. His fellow members were so moved by what he said of the sufferings of his co-religionists in Europe that when he had finished they all rose to their feet in mute expression of their sympathy: an almost unknown happening in the House.

Late in 1944, Mr. Churchill offered him the post of Under-Secretary to the Ministry of Supply, which he held until May 1945. Alas, by then, a new anxiety governed our lives; the sight in his one remaining eye began to fail.

But I have run ahead of time: in 1935 both my parents-in-law had died within a year of each other and a proportion of their possessions had devolved on my husband. A year later an avalanche of wooden crates containing furniture, pictures, china and *objets d'art* of all kinds descended on us in a house already full of appropriate beauty. I shall never forget our embarrassment on surveying this problem. In the event, incorporation proved much easier than I had expected, as fortunately the tastes of my parents-in-law and of the previous owners of Waddesdon were in such harmony that the difficulties of re-arrangement were greatly minimised.

We had just got all the things from Paris settled in their new quarters when the war clouds appeared in 1938 and, at the time of Munich, the contents of the house were dismantled and put in the cellar for safety. In that year they did not remain below ground for long, but we began seriously to think of what to do should war really come.

Our first idea was a hospital and we invited an official from the Ministry of Health to 'case the joint' with that end in view. His verdict was disappointing: 'the most unsuitable house for a hospital which could be imagined'. We came to understand that *boiserie*, even if covered up, would be a first-class harbourer of germs, and so we had to give up that idea. After many consultations, the only function it was deemed we could

Wartime at Waddesdon

118

The children having their
afternoon rest

usefully attempt, was to harbour children from the perils of air
attack on London. In the event, three separate organisations
from Croydon, caring for one hundred children in all, and all
under five years of age, were selected for Waddesdon. We were
greatly relieved to hear the children would be accompanied by
their attendant nurses and their own furniture.

By Easter 1939 one of the most odious consequences of
Hitler's rule over Germany had a direct impact on life in
Waddesdon village. His anti-Jewish drive was making existence
in Germany intolerable for all Jews—neither age, youth nor
any previous outstanding service for Germany made any

120

Sitting on the stairs on which King Edward VII, when Prince of Wales, broke his leg in 1898

difference. Our young cousin, Lord Rothschild was active in trying to arrange for the evacuation of Jews from Germany and he told us of the plight of a Jewish Orphanage in Frankfort a/Main which urgently needed to be moved to England. It was run by a most capable couple, Dr. and Mrs. Steinhardt who also had two young daughters of their own and an adult sister-in-law. The whole group numbered thirty; the ages of the orphans varied between six and twelve.

Luckily a large house in the village had been built and planned by Miss Alice as a maternity home to be run by two nurses who had looked after her admirably during one of her

121

illnesses. By 1939 both nurses had died and the house was available for the Orphanage, and just big enough to house the refugees. They arrived for Easter and remained in this house called 'The Cedars' until all the children had grown up and found careers for themselves all over the world. It says much for the understanding of the village, and for the tact of the new-comers, that this little orphanage was welcomed with open arms. The children were all educated either in the village school or in the Grammar School in Aylesbury. They learnt English astonishingly quickly and were integrated into the life of the village almost immediately. They were not only quick to learn but also proved their worth on the playing field: football came naturally to them and one boy even represented Aylesbury in a boxing contest.

They are now scattered all over the world, in England, Israel, Canada and North and South America. Their careers are diverse; one is the Assistant Agent to a big estate in England; another, also in England, is a Master baker. One is the head green-keeper at the Caesarea golf-course in Israel and others are lawyers, writers and industrialists in a variety of countries. During the war they were unfailingly helpful: the Waddesdon village Salvage Collection record reached dizzy heights thanks to the regularity of their assistance and their persuasiveness.

Three days after the declaration of war, our 100 'under-fives' with their escorts and furniture duly arrived. We had been given four days' notice to prepare for them, but thanks to the rehearsal at the time of Munich, this went much more smoothly than could have been hoped. With the exception of three rooms on the ground floor, all the others were stripped and emptied, as were all the bedrooms on the first floor. We ourselves were evacuated to the Bachelors' Wing. There we and our household occupied the first and second floors and we shared the kitchen with the children.

The first few days were naturally somewhat chaotic, as the children came from three separate establishments in Croydon. Their three staffs were unknown to each other and unaccus-tomed to co-operation, being used to their own routines. It took a little time to persuade them to combine their hours for food.

Ultimately the Croydon contingents were recalled in 1942 and found other quarters which suited them better than those we could offer. They were immediately replaced by the Minis-try of Health which sent us 100 children all belonging to a single unit in the care of Miss Ridley who was the epitome of calm kindness and understanding of both young and old.

The picture of life at Waddesdon during the second World War was little different from that of any other rural area which

122

was in a relatively targetless zone. Our only strange distinction was that throughout the war, although subject to 'black-out' like everyone else, a beacon blazed throughout the night on top of the Manor, to prevent aircraft crashing into it as they came in to land at Westcott airfield, just to the north. But the war, of course, affected everybody's life in one way or another. Even those who were not fighting or making things for offensive or defensive use, were jolted out of their routine. Apart from the children in the Manor, many other evacuees were housed in the village. In addition, the garden bothy became a temporary shelter for 'expectant mothers', and the Village Hall, no doubt much to its surprise ,was occupied for nearly two years by families whose numbers at times rose to nearly one hundred persons: they slept there, and were fed there from a canteen in an adjoining room where a team of women from the village cooked for them seven days a week, and week after week, and month after month.

Then in 1941, Waddesdon Park became one of the biggest petrol dumps in the country. Naturally, there was not a drop for us, and it was hard not to feel covetous: there was not a sizeable tree within our boundaries which did not have a concrete platform and a Nissen hut full of petrol drums nestling beneath it.

I was the local WVS Organiser and mercilessly badgered everyone in the neighbourhood to collect salvage or make camouflage nets, in addition to trying to cope with all the bits and pieces connected with those elastic words 'Evacuation' and 'Civil Defence'.

There was one other occasion in which Waddesdon's protective capacity was tested for yet another purpose. This need arose in 1944, during the Doodle Bug period which, in its early stages, caused considerable damage in London before brilliant counter-measures were invented.

Lady Reading, Chairman of WVS, whose Headquarters in Tothill Street were situated in rather an obvious target area close to Westcott, Downing Street and Buckingham Palace, became anxious for the safety of the very mixed but precious stores housed on the premises. These included a huge variety of invaluable gifts from the USA; emergency supplies for the bombed out; canteen equipment and a stock of stationery which, at that time of paper shortage, was particularly prized.

Lady Reading asked me if I could still find a cranny at Waddesdon where these miscellaneous objects could be stored away. Fortunately, the stables were largely filled with varied junk which could be exposed to the weather. Maria Brassey was the WVS member at Tothill Street in charge of all stores;

Lady Reading having accepted our proferred hospitality, despatched her in a 3-ton lorry, brimming over with its load. She continued to drive it down several times a week, until even the Waddesdon accommodation could take no more. At the time this invasion did not seem specially notable, but good fortune sometimes reaches one unannounced. The driver of that appallingly noisy lorry has since become an invaluable friend who has proved, ever since 1944 that a ready wit, a sense of humour and a temperament that nothing daunts can help in trials and tribulations, and they have engendered a sanity which might well have deserted me but for her companionship. When I was confronted with problems and complications, she developed a special capacity for coping with them which was as astonishing as it remains welcome.

The wonderful moment when war in Europe came to an end brought WVS the most enchanting of all jobs they had been asked to undertake. It was decided that many of our prisoners of war, as they were liberated, should be flown from the German camps direct to Westcott airfield. Most of those arriving appeared with their uniforms in tatters, or at least well below the army standard of smartness. The Army therefore decreed that none of the returning prisoners should be allowed to leave the airfield for their own homes until they had been newly kitted out. New uniforms themselves were supplied by the army, but would not be complete until they had had sown on to them the regimental or corps insignia, medals or stripes of rank proper to each man. I was asked ' Could the WVS come and sew? ' Throughout those days and warm summer nights women were gathered in from all the surrounding villages. They sat at trestle tables on the airfield, sewing away for dear life, often by the light of hurricane lamps, so that each man could go to his longed-for home at the earliest possible moment. As they sewed, they talked to the men whose uniforms they were embellishing, in the first enchanted hour of their return.

A shockingly untimely attack of chicken-pox deprived me of this personal pleasure but I was nevertheless kept busy in my bed, arranging on the telephone the many rotas of sempstresses and their transport to their enviable duty.

I think Miss Ridley's Nursery, which had succeeded the Croydon contingents, were sad to leave Waddesdon and we were really sorry to see them go. There are two images of the children's stay with us which will always remain in my mind: the first, seeing them being carried down the winding staircase to their prepared beds in the basement during an air-raid warning—all so orderly and quiet and, to a strange degree, so natural. And then the Christmases the children spent at Wad-

desdon. The house never looked so attractive as when they all assembled in the East Gallery, and the door of the Breakfast Room was suddenly flung open revealing a huge lit-up Christmas Tree, with a live Father Christmas to greet them and hand out gifts. This imposing personage was none other than my beloved maid, Eliza Kimber who, sweltering in the appropriate beard and robes, undertook this exhausting role for the duration.

After the 1945 General Election, when Jimmy lost his seat for the Isle of Ely in the House of Commons, he went through another period of poor health, partly due to injuries from an accidental fall he had had during the election campaign. There was, however, one advantage in this phase of our existence— we were able to spend much more time at Waddesdon and could take stock of our surroundings.

We had been immensely fortunate that nearly all the contents of Waddesdon had escaped irretrievable damage during the war. There were only two near misses. In the first week of the war we had put all the pictures in the cellar in specially fitted wooden cases made by our house-carpenter, Mr. Chapman. Fortunately, after a fortnight, he thought he would open one or two of the cases just to see that the pictures inside were all right. To his horror, in case after case, he found a blue haze creeping over the surface of each canvas or panel. Expert consultants told us that the only hope was to remove all the pictures from their damp confinement in the cellar and expose them to fresh air. Luckily, the Grey Drawing-room was still available; racks were made and installed there, and the pictures hoisted into them. There were three pictures by Watteau which never quite regained their former condition, but all the rest responded to the fresh air treatment. We comforted ourselves with the thought that the danger of Hitler's bombs falling on Waddesdon was less than the known peril of Waddesdon damp. However, when we received an invitation from the National Gallery of Ottowa, we availed ourselves of their kindness, and thankfully sent them four pictures for the duration of the war. In Ottowa they were admirably housed and exhibited in safety and returned to us, when peace came, in excellent condition.

The other misadventure occurred on the very last day of the war. In the general relief and excitement a tap was left running in a bathroom on the first floor, and the resultant flood cascaded down into one of the three rooms we had retained for the storage of furniture. A stream of water fell plumb onto the pictorial marquetry of the writing table given by his friends to Beaumarchais in 1781, and spread from there to a pile of books which were also stored in the Baron's Room. The results were alarming, particularly to the table, but this was found to be reparable through the skill of Messrs. Hatfield's *ébénistes*.

Following the departure of the children we were confronted with the problem of what to do with the house. Shortages of every sort in the post-war period included a shortage of personnel and the idea of re-instating Waddesdon for us two old people seemed out of the question. But something had to be done: we could not leave all the contents of the house in a few rooms, stacked up to the ceiling. It was, in fact, quite difficult to enter the Morning Room it was so congested; only a mouse had managed to do so, and had established a tiny trail right across the room, getting what nourishment it could on the way.

It was then that the solution of the National Trust began to germinate in my husband's mind and I cannot say how thankful I am that it did. But before the Trust could even be approached there would have to be something visible to show

Girl at a window by Gerard Dou, bought by Baron Ferdinand from the Six van Hillegom Collection in 1897

126

them, so we decided to unpack everything in store and re-instate the ground floor rooms.

On examining these rooms, now clear of the cots and minia ture tables and chairs to which we had become so accustomed, we found that they did, indeed, bear some scars of war. However these, needless to say, were all well below waist level. The Red Drawing Room whose walls were covered in silk, had been the children's dining room, so may have been specially vulnerable to sticky fingers; its walls had also been a tempting background for coloured chalks. Anyone who has had the experience of trying to remove the traces of coloured chalk from any surface—from natural fibre to marble—will know what a frustrating occupation it can be. But the worst damage to the red damask came from the sunshine that had poured into that room unimpeded, and rotted its lovely panels into rags. It would clearly have to be replaced.

We searched high and low for a material with a pattern which would suit the dimensions of the room, realising as we did so, ever more clearly, the degree of perfection achieved by Baron Ferdinand in his choice of materials. Nothing we could find equalled what was now in tatters, and we were fortunate in eventually discovering that Messrs. Hammond employed a superb weaver aged 81 who could faithfully reproduce the the Baron's wall-covering. Messrs. Hammond found this commission so unusual that, with our gratified consent, they affixed a brass plate to the wall, under the new silk, on which were inscribed the names of all those who had worked on the weaving and on the cutting, sewing and application of the new silk to the walls. The final name on this plate was that of Mrs. Green, our housekeeper, the very remarkable successor to Mrs. Boxall. Perhaps in some future age, this plate will be revealed and will become an object of interest to some art historian. But however assiduous a researcher he may be, I feel sure that he will never be able to recreate in his thesis the personality of Mrs. Green. Red-haired, formidable, an unmistakable member of the old school, but with a heart of gold, she was altogether wonderful, both to us and for Waddesdon. It is difficult to separate her name from that of her boon companion, Mabel Chatfield, the Linen Maid, whose character can only be described as angelic. Whenever Mrs Green and I, in our household perplexities, had a divergence of opinion and she wished to be assured that her own view would prevail, her final and nearly always winning thrust of argument was to restate her opinion and add 'And Mabel thinks so too'. I believe if they had known the house better Messrs. Hammond would also have added Mabel's name to that plaque as well as that of the other pillar of war-time Waddesdon, Mr. Tissot, who had cooked every one of the meals eaten by the children in that very room.

It was curiously difficult to replace the furniture as it had been before the war; I kept on getting mixed up in my mind with the arrangement before and after my parents-in-law's possessions had appeared from Paris. Moreover, although the exact angle and spacing of furniture can make or mar a room, much of the furniture at Waddesdon is heavy enough to prohibit many experiments to find out the best arrangement. I remember my joy when I suddenly realised that the carpets still bore the slight marks of flattened pile made by the legs of tables and cupboards which had stood on them before 1939. No longer was replacement a question of 'fish and find out'; one had only to search for those slight indentations on the carpet, retrieve the piece of furniture which corresponded to them and lower it gently into place.

Negotiations were started with the National Trust and we decided to transfer ourselves to Eythrope which Miss Alice had left to my husband with the Waddesdon Estate. As we had no use for the Pavilion at Eythrope in 1922, it had been let to Mrs. Somerset Maugham who, unlike Miss Alice, had a need for bedrooms and bathrooms. She therefore added what became known as the 'Maugham Wing' and lived there until the war. It then had other tenants, but now it was vacant again, although in great need of repair.

In the immediate post-war years London and many other cities needed rebuilding and in order that the whole construction force of the country should concentrate on repairing bomb-damage, the ordinary private householder was restricted to doing building and decorating work of only £25 in value each year, unless he was given a special licence. For some time it seemed most unlikely that we should ever receive a licence, but then the roof of the 'Maugham Wing' fell in and so demolished the only bedrooms the house possessed. As this made it uninhabitable, a building licence was forthcoming in the mid 1950's and the work could be started. But all this had taken a long time and on May 7th, 1957, Jimmy died, before Eythrope, which is now my home, was ready for occupation.

During his last years, when he was out of the House of Commons and struggling against blindness and ill health, Jimmy had never ceased to work for the causes he had supported throughout his adult life. To the end of his days he remained a convinced member of the Liberal party and was constantly in touch with its leaders. He kept himself remarkably well-informed about world politics, but his most constant preoccupation remained the fate and development of the State of Israel. He consistently advocated the possibility of including Jewish Palestine in a larger configuration—in fact, the British Empire—and thus, in some measure, securing a lasting peace in the Middle East: but only shortly before his death the Foreign Office was still brushing any such proposal aside. This is not the place to refer to his specific achievements in Israel; they are dealt with in detail in Simon Schama's *Two Rothschilds and the Land of Israel*.

After Jimmy's death a number of people wrote to *The Times* about him: most of them were far more capable than I of putting their memories into words. One of them wrote:

' Young men and women had only to spend a few moments with him to forget his age and distinction and to treat him as a stimulating and provocative contemporary. They would not have guessed that when he was a young man he left Paris and spent a year in Australia, under an assumed name to find out what it was like not to be called Rothschild '.

The author of another contribution was particularly apt in describing Jimmy's character. He wrote:

' James de Rothschild was at all periods of his life a man of striking distinction and charm and spirit, with a most brilliant and penetrating wit, a rich and eccentric fancy and ideas of great sweep and originality. His conversation was entrancing, fed by a prodigious memory and an all-embracing curiosity and a fabulous insight into human motives and character; an acute sense of the comical and incongruous; a love of life, of paradox, of anything new and original; an often diabolical ingenuity in argument which he could conduct in three languages with which he appeared to be equally familiar. He was a most fascinating and indeed magnetic figure to his friends.

Violently proud, morally fastidious, with a deep natural piety, he was devoted to the tradition of his family, his faith, his race and his adopted country. He was first and foremost a *Grand Seigneur*, formidable, imperious, disdainful, contemptuous of danger; civilised with extreme independence of character and judgment, and with a deeply imaginative and unswerving loyalty to the political causes he served, especially Liberalism and Zionism, to both of which his life was devoted ... His broken health forced him towards the end to lead the life of a semi-invalid, but his vitality and vast interest in people and events remained unimpaired. Conversation with him obliterated all differences of age and reputation. The combination of paternalistic and benevolent schemes, of

130

romantic loyalties, gaiety, the verve, the high originality,
the style of life and utterances belonged to a world of
which he was one of the most noble and attractive
survivors'.

The day after Jimmy's death a popular newspaper sent one
of their reporters to Waddesdon. He spent his time sitting in
one or other of the village public houses, offering each habitué,
as he entered, a glass of beer and £10 down for any story he
cared to tell about my husband. I am told that all the reporter
received were stony stares, and that he eventually retreated to
London without a story of any kind, and with all his money
intact. The beer drinkers of Waddesdon were, it seems, at one
with *The Times* which, in its official obituary, had described
Jimmy as 'an ideal landlord, a squire of the best type'.

Quite apart from my personal feelings, the sudden change for
me from an existence which had been totally free from taking
decisions of importance, was traumatic. My husband had indeed been the guiding light in all sections of my life, and now
the struggle began to try to take the decisions which he would
have taken and to act in accordance with what I thought would
have been his wishes.

He had intended to make Waddesdon over to the National
Trust in his life time; now it came to them by bequest. I under-

131

stand the Trust had some hesitation in accepting it not only because the house was relatively modern, but also because it was built and furnished in the French style. At least one influential member of the National Trust, the late Lord Esher, declared quite plainly 'I hate French furniture', and for some days Waddesdon's fate hung in the balance. I think in the end Lord Crawford, who was then Chairman of the National Trust, persuaded his colleagues that perhaps the contents of the house might compensate for the drawbacks of its foreign style and relative modernity. In any case, it was realised that thanks to the endowment my husband had bequeathed with the house, its maintenance would not cost the Trust anything.

Curiously enough an argument did arise with the Treasury over the endowment. Like all those settled on houses bequeathed to the National Trust, it would be exempt from death duty. But the Treasury held the view, at first, that the endowment for Waddesdon was bigger than would be needed for its upkeep, and thought therefore it should be taxable. Fortunately, the Treasury changed its mind and experience has shown very clearly that the amount needed to maintain Waddesdon had been correctly gauged by its donor, but only thanks to wise subsequent investment.

If it be true that the best way of keeping grief under control is to be forced to be very busy, the Estate Duty Office of the Inland Revenue must indeed be the widow's best friend.

In this century, whenever someone dies, a valuation has to be made of all their possessions so that the Estate Duty Office can assess the amount of death duty payable. Any of their possessions, however, which are judged to be of a standard which would be acceptable to a national museum can be classified as being of 'National interest' and, if the new owner agrees to keep such objects in good and safe condition, no duty is payable until such time as a decision is taken to sell them. When Miss Alice died in 1922 a probate inventory had been made of all the contents of Waddesdon and Eythrope which filled five sizeable volumes, and many of the objects listed in them were of 'National interest'. It was now my task to find, identify and make available for the inspection of museum officials all those things which we had agreed in 1922 to keep in good and safe condition.

Most of the objects Jimmy had left to the National Trust were relatively easy to identify by comparing descriptions in the old inventories with what was now visible in the newly arranged ground floor rooms. But the arms collected by Miss Alice to replace some of the objects left by her brother to the British Museum presented far greater problems. At a guess,

132

I could distinguish a halberd from a rapier and, perhaps, an arquebus from a pistol, but my lack of knowledge was total when it came to identifying, say, 'A pillow sword enriched with gold azzima' or 'A main gauche with chased drooping quillons'. In the end I was forced to disregard these cryptic descriptions in the old inventories. I counted all the cutting instruments I could see, all the fire arms and all the powder flasks and, when these were found to tally in number with those listed in 1922, I left it at that. Fortunately, the Estate Duty Office and the National Trust, the new owner of the arms, pronounced themselves satisfied.

My lack of specialised knowledge also bedevilled the identification of garden statuary. We had so often walked by marble figures and vases thinking how beautiful they looked dappled with the play of light and shade through the trees. But now I was confronted with the problem of deciding whether a large nude marble lady peering from her leafy bower was indeed 'Pomona—18th century', 'Flora—probably Venetian', or 'Ceres—19th century'. I learnt the hard way that it all depended on what produce she happened to be carrying. A similar state of indecision seized me when confronted by large muscular stone gentlemen. I took it that if they were clasping rather agitated females they were probably the *Rape of the Sabines* or *Pluto carrying off Proserpine*, but

Dutch musical box
surmounted by a flute
player: late eighteenth
century

Waddesdon seen through the North Fountain and framed by an avenue of oaks and cedars, *Atlantica glauca*

if they were not, who was to say which was Hercules and which was Samson?

The upper floors at Waddesdon were the most difficult of all. The contents of all the rooms which had been cleared for the children were either still packed away higgeldy-piggeldy in any attic cupboard or cranny which could be made to hold them, or else had come out of the main store rooms into unaccustomed and unlikely places. Daily, hugging the old inventories—or as many of them as I could carry—I tramped the house, trying to find and identify, and incidentally make up my mind what would be best for me to take to Eythrope, all of whose contents had been in store at Waddesdon ever since the Pavilion had been let. I remember particularly searching for a 'National interest' object described in 1922 as 'A musical box—probably Dutch'. Vainly I searched in every cupboard and drawer for any small box-like object. Memory plays strange tricks and I cannot now recall what it was that

135

one day inspired me to consider a ten foot high carved wooden statue on a plinth, of a young man playing a flute. Had he, perhaps, the musical connection we were seeking? Investigation proved that there was indeed a mechanism for making music in the plinth, and that this was, at last, the long sought musical box. Because of its vast size, it had been left undisturbed throughout the war and stood where I had always remembered it in a corner of the long bedroom corridor.

This was the season of lists. Every evening they had to be compiled for the National Trust; for the Estate Duty Office; for the various museum experts who would be coming to check all the 'National interest' objects; for the packers who would be removing me to Eythrope as soon as it became habitable. There were even yet more lists to be made in connection with, for me, a most untimely County Council election in which I had to defend my seat.

Finally everything, as I thought, was located, labelled and entered on the appropriate list. But I had reckoned without the impeccable precision of the Estate Duty Office officials who compared the many sheets I sent them with the probate lists of 1922 which they had on their files. Their reply to my final definitive effort on their behalf, instead of acknowledging in any way the hours of work it represented, merely stated that I appeared to have omitted two items which had been recorded in 1922. The first, they said, was: 'Fountain composed of three groups of tritons, nereids and marine monsters' and the second—'Small tapestry cushion with motif of heraldic lion'. Happily repairing these omissions did not mean much more searching. The North Fountain, at the end of the approach to the house, was so large that it had been overlooked and the tapestry cushion had been duly found, but through a typing error, had been left off the list.

At this time too, Mademoiselle Denise André arrived at Waddesdon to inspect all the things bequeathed to the National Trust and repair and clean them in any way necessary so that they might be handed over in tip-top condition. The André family had played a part at Waddesdon since the days when old M. André, Mademoiselle André's grandfather, had helped Baron Ferdinand with the decoration of his 'new smoking room' in the 1880's. Monsieur André *grandpère* had been the head of the family firm in Paris which was famous for repairing works of art of all kinds. Their secrets of how to clean safely, or mend invisibly, objects made of porcelain, ormolu, stone, wood or tortoiseshell were known, it seems, to few others. The grandson of the founder—Mademoiselle André's brother—had unhappily, died young, leaving a number

Late 16th century Bohemian glass beaker painted with the 'Ages of Man'.

Overleaf 6-fold Savonnerie screen woven on designs by A. F. Desportes between 1720 and 1740.

136

of small children, and it was left to his sister and his widow to carry on the firm until the children became old enough to play their part. Mademoiselle André, living in Paris, and working in museums and great collections throughout Europe, was the most cultured and charming of human beings, and had magic in her fingers; it was a delight to watch her handling any work of art. She also had one unexpected talent—an extraordinary sympathy with animals of all kinds which every species reciprocated.

When Mademoiselle André came to Waddesdon which, except for the war years, she did at regular intervals, the crustiest old parrot in the aviary would start dancing on his perch and the shyest inmate of the deer pens would come galloping at her call. To the discomfort of late sleepers, a cockatoo, rightly named Denis the Menace, who should have lived in the aviary but who was more often at liberty, would fly to the house in the early morning when Mademoiselle André was present and would sit on a chimney, screaming down it, until such time as she opened her window, and invited him in to have breakfast with her. But her greatest love affair was with Jumbo, a guard dog who lived in a large kennel by the back door. She always spoke to him in French, addressing him as 'Joombeau'. Together they would go for walks while she told him the latest news of poodles and bull-dogs of her acquaintance in Paris.

Jumbo died not long after my husband's death and I fear that at that time none of us thought of letting Mademoiselle André know of this sad event, which she only discovered on her next visit. The distress she felt made her guilty—I am sure for the first and only time—of expressing her ideas in what was, perhaps, a less than tactful order. I could not be at Waddesdon the day she arrived on this occasion, but on reaching home the next morning I sought her out and I remember her running towards me, crying as she did so: 'Ah! Madame, comme c'est triste! Pas de Joombeau! Pas de Monsieur de Rothschild!'

Mademoiselle André, alas, is now also dead. But before she left this world she handed on to her nephew Jean-Michel her knowledge and her expertise and he, with Pierre Klieski and other talented colleagues, continue to come to Waddesdon for the National Trust and take those stitches in time which, it is hoped, will preserve old works of art for the enjoyment of many future generations.

The front door at Waddesdon.

The National Trust

My HUSBAND'S BEQUEST to the National Trust consisted of the house; 120 acres of surrounding land; the contents of the eleven ground floor rooms and all the arms and the garden statuary.

Lord Crawford immediately proposed that a National Trust Management Committee for Waddesdon should be formed and was kind enough to suggest that I should be its Chairman. One of the most sensitive features of the National Trust's policy is that, so far as possible, the family of a donor should either be encouraged to continue to live in the house, or help to keep it in the tradition to which it had been accustomed.

It may perhaps interest some people to know what preparations we thought it necessary to make at Waddesdon before it could be opened to the public.

We were somewhat harassed at the time by one of the national newspapers which kept on printing paragraphs asking why my husband's bequest was still invisible to the public, some months after his death. It was even suggested that there must be some mysterious circumstance which still kept the contents of Waddesdon hidden. The only mystery lay in the newspaper's lack of comprehension of what had to be done before we could open the house. It was still alive with museum experts who came on behalf of the Estate Duty Office whenever their ordinary work allowed and they were constantly running into valuers who were assessing all the more mundane furniture and things such as sheets and saucepans, bedsteads and hoovers, on which duty would be payable. At the same time the house was full of workmen because the Management Committee's first job was to make the house and its contents as secure as possible. As I was about to move to Eythrope it was obvious that others would have to be found to live in the Manor at Waddesdon permanently. The problem was how to ensure a comfortable family life for a number of resident wardens in a house which was in no way designed for that purpose. The answer was to carve out individual flats, each with its own front door, and complete with bedrooms, sitting-room, kitchen and bathroom. This was a very big conversion

The author, photographed at Eythrope, by Bern Schwartz in 1977

job which naturally took time; it was brilliantly carried out by our ingenious architect, Mr. R. J. Page.

It also took time to recruit the wardens and several of those who agreed to come could not leave their previous jobs immediately. Perhaps thanks to the comfortable modern flats which were made for them, the house has been fully manned since 1958 and most of our wardens remain with us until they retire. Some of them then find accommodation in Waddesdon village and continue to help by lending a hand from time to time.

The vital need was to find people able and willing to take on a great variety of tasks. Security was one thing, but keep and cleanliness came next on the list of essentials. Mrs. Green and Mabel Chatfield had more than reached the age of retirement and when I left, they decided they would also leave. How on earth could they be replaced?

As so often in my difficulties I turned to Lady Reading for advice. Her response was immediate. I was bidden to luncheon to meet the head of the WAAF. On learning of my problem she told me of Miss Gwyneth Morgan who, during the war, had been in charge of a large WAAF camp in Wales. Since leaving the service she had been living in another house, recently bequeathed to the National Trust, where she had been helping the widow of the donor who, for personal reasons, wished to pack up and move to another house. In doing so, it appeared, Miss Morgan had won the praise and gratitude of all. Now knowing what such a feat implied, I was most anxious to meet one who appeared to have experience both in taking charge of others and in handling works of art. I made Miss Morgan's acquaintance and took to her at once; I was indeed glad when she agreed to come to Waddesdon as its housekeeper.

Mrs. Green was exceedingly doubtful of anyone lacking a life-time's education in 'private service' being able to look after the contents of Waddesdon satisfactorily. It was not quite a case of 'Mabel thinking so too' but very nearly. However Miss Morgan arrived some months before Mrs. Green and Mabel left. They told her all they knew and initiated her into the so-called mysteries of 'the Waddesdon standard' and how to attain it. To their surprise she was so intelligently capable of absorbing their tuition that, when the day came, they left with lighter hearts and higher hopes for the future of Waddesdon than they had ever thought possible. For some years Miss Morgan demonstrated her ability to recruit willing helpers from the village; train those who had not worked in the house before, and maintain the 'keep and care' in the tradition established by Miss Alice. When the time came for Miss

140

Morgan to wish to retire she handed this tradition on to her immediate successor, and so far the chain has remained unbroken ever since.

The choice of a Director to be in over-all charge at Waddesdon was one of the most important decisions the Management Committee had to take in 1957. We interviewed twelve candidates who came with their wives to look and be looked at. We chose as Director a nationally known figure with a great artistic reputation. Unfortunately it soon became clear he was not really interested in the period or taste of the contents and decoration of Waddesdon and he and the Management Committee found themselves in constant disagreement. It was with mingled disappointment and regret that we accepted his resignation not long after the house was opened to the public. Looking back on this unhappy time, when sympathy between us seemed impossible to attain, I feel sure that his love of modern art, of which Waddesdon was devoid, would have always made it uncongenial to him.

After a few months experience we believed we understood what would be the most desirable qualities in an administrator at Waddesdon. He should possess such things as a flair for man and woman management; an understanding of the best temperature and humidity for pictures and furniture; an ability to spot a leak in a roof or a boiler; even a comprehension of the part hoggin can play in avenues over which coaches thunder. He should also have rather more than a nodding acquaintance with the mysteries of composing annual estimates. In our search for such a paragon we turned to the Army and were extremely fortunate. First a Brigadier set a pattern of good management and when, ten years later, he retired, he was followed by a Colonel; both proved to have all these abilities as well as many other virtues.

Maybe it is coincidence, but Brigadier N. S. Cowan and Colonel A. R. Waller, both regular soldiers who had had distinguished military carreers in war and in peace, developed an intuitive feeling and love for works of art although in their previous lives they had had nothing to do with their keep or arrangement. Happily they both also proved to be admirable PRO's—a talent not to be ignored in the management of National Trust properties. Last but not least, both came accompanied by the most charming of wives who, each in her turn, has taken in her stride the duties of 'instant hostess' to visiting experts and has provided that oil and comfort which is so needed when some crisis hits the lives of those who inhabit a closed community. Their handiwork is also in evidence at Waddesdon. Mrs. Cowan evolved at lightning speed

Madame de Pompadour, signed and dated J.-B. Lemoyne, 1761

Opposite The Blue Sèvres room. The lacquer and ormolu mechanical clock in the form of a birdcage, which includes a musical box, was made in Switzerland, c. 1780

the tented ceiling of the display of materials in the 'Store Room'—a problem which had defeated both our architect and decorator; and Mrs. Waller's talent for cleaning the miniature silver on display is only equalled by her intimate and soothing influence on the birds in the aviary.

It had always been Jimmy's special wish that the general appearance of Waddesdon would give visitors the impression of an inhabited private house rather than a museum. It had indeed been a most convenient setting for a house party of a couple of dozen people but it was another matter to adapt it for the hundreds we hoped might visit us simultaneously once the house was open to the public. All the sitting rooms

143

The 'Store Room'

Opposite Two terra-cotta figures by Clodion. Late eighteenth century

had comfortable armchairs made by Howard, a fashionable upholsterer who, alas, vanished after the first world war. Now that we hoped each room would be filled with many visitors a choice had to be made; there would not be room for beautiful 18th century chairs, the modern armchairs and the public, and it was the comfortable chairs and sofas which had to be sacrificed. Old photographs taken before they were removed show how immensely liveable the house looked, even if a little more crowded. There was one other obvious difficulty in keeping things as they were—the Savonnerie carpets; they looked beautiful in many of the rooms, but how could we keep visiting feet from treading on them? We solved this problem by stretching in front of them thin coloured cord supported on slim stands only about one foot high. This is what Monsieur Pierre Verlet of the Louvre calls '*protection symbolique*' and so far it has worked admirably.

Circulation was also another matter to be considered. Inevitably at Waddesdon there would be no way of avoiding one

144

line of arriving visitors meeting another line going away, until we could arrange for some of the first floor rooms to be opened and thus provide a circular tour and an unencumbered exit. There are many methods of showing visitors round a house, some more agreeable than others. Freedom to roam with information available whenever it is desired is delightful but costly to administer. Waiting for some twenty people to collect and then conducting them round, opening and locking all doors as the party progresses, is economical and secure, but not quite so pleasant. But there are many ways which can be devised between these two extremes in different houses. At Waddesdon, on each open day, we find it necessary, in addition to the resident staff, to have some forty extra people on duty inside and outside the house.

Most sightseers expect to be able to buy a guide-book of some sort: getting one written, illustrated and printed introduced us to the problems of book production about which we were to learn much more when the detailed catalogues of the contents of the house began to be published some years later.

Before the house was ready for opening we plied the National Trust with innumerable questions of a practical nature—what would they suggest we should prepare in the way of parking

Waddesdon during the
'open' season

facilities, food, lavatories and litter bins? As far as the last were concerned we received an answer which surprised us. The ideal, apparently, would be to keep the garden looking like a private one rather than a public park furnished with expectant receptacles for refuse. In some magical way this has also worked so far—no litter bins mean no litter.

All these preparations took almost a year to complete. I was obliged, because of the Probate, to continue to live at Waddesdon for nearly all that time, so there was no need to engage any but a skeleton staff before I left. This meant that a large part of one year's income from the endowment was available to cover some of the cost of the structural alterations.

Just before we opened the then Minister of Works came to Waddesdon for a preview. After a careful tour, he very kindly told us not to be disappointed if the attendance of visitors dropped dramatically following the interest a new venture always attracted. I am thankful to say that the reverse has happened. After a rather shaky start when fewer than 30,000 came, the number of our visitors increased year by year until in 1974 there were some 103,000. In the last four years our figures have fluctuated just below or just above the 100,000 mark, and with this we are content. We have discovered how helplessly dependent we are on the weather, particularly on Bank Holidays; in the last few years they have been capable of producing snow, thunder and intense heat.

In one way we may well have disappointed our visitors. In our over-riding anxiety to protect the contents of Waddesdon we made a rule, and have kept to it, that children under the age of 12 should not be admitted to the house. I believe we are almost alone in trying to enforce this, but as I have explained, the house is arranged as nearly as possible as if it could be inhabited at any moment, and this necessarily means that there are many precious china and other fragile objects within easy, breakable reach. The visual result, we believe, greatly enhances the pleasure of visitors. But it takes a good hour to go round Waddesdon and for small children it is no pleasure to be kept under tight control for such a time; and a struggle between conscientious parents and fractious, thwarted children is a risk we are not prepared to take. Children are most welcome in the garden, the aviary and the tea-room—as they will be in a special outdoor play ground which is now being planned for them, which we hope may provide distraction for them while their parents are enjoying a tour of the house.

Once Waddesdon was opened, it settled into its summer and winter routines—both equally busy, but quite different. From Easter until the end of October all efforts are concentrated on

148

The State bedroom, now transformed to show examples of Sèvres china of every colour in the house. The Savonnerie carpet was made for the Grande Galerie at the Louvre, c. 1681. The Beauvais tapestry on the sofa is mid-18th century

Overleaf A lace fan which belonged to Baroness Ferdinand

Three eighteenth century fans from Baroness Edmond's collection

seeing our visitors get everything they want; a convenient place to park; an enjoyable tour of the house; any information they ask for; guide-books, postcards or catalogues; and a good tea. Naturally the provision of all these things implies a large staff and the Manor has become, to some extent, the Waddesdon village industry. Neighbours who have an interest in the arts form a changing rota of guides; they have all been subjected to a rigorous training which enables them to answer intelligently questions about any object in the house. We rather pride ourselves that they can do so in at least four European languages. As the guides' work is necessarily seasonal, we try to hold their interest during the winter by arranging lectures for them by experts or by planning special visits to other collections. When the house is open it is not only the guides who are on duty: the bus plies to and from the village bringing in sellers of postcards and garden produce; makers and servers of tea and, most numerous of all, the 'sitting wardens'. These merely sit in each room the public go through, guarding its contents. They seldom have to prevent attempted theft, but are often called on to frustrate a desire to touch.

Before we opened we were told horrifying stories of other houses where it was said china vases had to be filled with

149

lead or sand, or even bolted to the furniture on which they stood, to prevent their being rushed at and up-ended by enthusiasts who were anxious to see what marks the china bore. We have, I believe, found other means of protection and, in the event, have been free of such dangerous 'connoisseurs'. But, as in all other houses, we have had to take precautions against the unconquerable urge of all females to touch materials which appeal to them. It appears to be an unbreakable law of nature that if a woman sees any pleasing stuff, particularly velvet, she must inevitably stroke it with her fingers. Doubtless she will assume that such a caress from her will do no harm, but when thousands of women think so, one after another, the result can be disastrous even to the most stalwart textile. We have found the answer is to sheathe all easily touchable materials in the finest possible net up to a height beyond which a woman's hand is unlikely to stray. If fine enough the net is either invisible, or at most gives the faintest misty tinge to the material underneath it, but it does deter and preserve.

The application of net is a winter job, as is so much else. As the last visitor leaves on the last day of October the packing up begins. China, snuff boxes and other small objects are put away; everything that can be be covered is swathed in a linen *housse* or in white or black tissue paper which prevents colour fading or metal tarnishing. The weight is taken off great curtains by propping them up on chairs and every object in the house is allowed to relax comfortably in a state of hibernation. But this is not true of its human inhabitants—for them the winter is a truly busy time.

One seems to find a small factory in operation at every turn in the house between November and March. Garden seats are being oiled or painted; chandeliers are being laboriously cleaned and the lighting of pictures examined and improved. The Dining Room is cleared and filled with long trestle tables at which work a marvellously gifted team of sempstresses which the bus now carries to and from the village. They not only reline curtains but also undertake much more complicated preservation work on various textiles in the house.

In these days when so many people are anxious to save their houses and their precious contents from the necessity of sale by showing them to the public, one is apt to forget the unavoidable back-room work which must be undertaken. A private householder can, perhaps, put off to some convenient time the repairs for which his house and possessions may stand in need, but if one is aiming to attract visitors who pay, and who look at everything with minute attention, every sign of deterioration

152

The dining room at
Waddesdon in winter,
converted into a
sewing-room

must be spotted as soon as possible and repaired, if it can be, in the few winter months before a new season begins.

Quite apart from the vulnerability of the roof, which owing to its exposure to the elements, is generally expected to need repair from time to time, there seems to be nothing in any house which is not liable to call for attention. Everything from electric wiring to clocks, and from furniture to drawings is lamentably subject to slight disintegration which only constant supervision and care will halt.

Apart from the André family we have enjoyed the help and counsel of many outside experts. Mr. John Fowler gave us his invaluable advice over the re-instatement of the first floor of the West Wing: both the Victoria and Albert Museum and Mrs. Finch at Hampton Court have performed miracles with textiles whose repair was beyond our capabilities and the watchful eyes of Professor Rees-Jones of the Courtauld Institute and Miss Seddon have detected any trouble with the pictures which they have then arranged to put right. In recent years all the Savonnerie carpets and screens have been cleaned—probably for the

153

Repairs being done to the
roof of Waddesdon

first time since they were made more than two hundred years ago—by Mr. Maurice's firm in Wigmore Street, and the brilliance of their original colour has now been restored.

We decided early on to improve the circulation in the house by opening some of the rooms on the first floor. They were all still in their war-time condition and, having been used as dormitories for the children, were in considerable need of 'refurbishing'.

We were told that any self-respecting stately home always provided a view of at least one bedroom and, if possible, a bathroom as, apparently, an added attraction. So we started on what proved to be an extensive programme, partly rehabilitation and partly improvisation, which eventually provided, as part of the visitors' tour, eleven other rooms for display. This took many years to complete.

Fortunately, there was no lack of material to be shown on

154

this floor. In addition to the furniture for the bedrooms which had been stored away, we had two other sources of supply from France. Part of Jimmy's inheritance from his parents had not reached us before the war started and having remained in Paris fell a prey to the Germans. Some of it had been taken by Goering for his own use, but luckily this particular batch had never been unpacked and had remained in the cases in which they had been put for transmission to Germany. These included my parents-in-law's incredible store of textiles of all kinds, and of all centuries, which they had found on their many travels and which Baroness Edmond had treasured in case any of the contents of her various houses needed repair or replacement. Then there were many works of art which had been officially recuperated; mostly from the Austrian salt-mines, by the allied team led by Mr. Rorimer of the Metropolitan Musem in New York which had been given the task of tracking down and retrieving as much allied property as possible, as soon as the war ended; their success in doing this, though not complete, was considerable.

One way and another the rooms on the first floor were repainted and became filled, some with beautiful things, some with objects with an interesting past history and some with relics of former glory.

We thought more than two bedrooms would bore even the most domesticated of our visitors and so decided to turn the rest into exhibition rooms, more or less in the museum manner. Some structural alterations were needed but these only became a major operation in the West Wing. Here, Mr. Page most ingeniously converted four bedrooms, two bathrooms and two large corridors into four exhibition rooms which Mr. Fowler, with impeccable taste, provided with curtains and carpets which do much to mitigate any museum atmosphere. There were many individual collections made by different members of the family, through the years, which we were able to show here: Miss Alice's Dutch dolls' house silver; my mother-in-law's lace and her eighteenth century buttons and seals and part of my father-in-law's famous collection of drawings. Here too, the lovely embroidered Chinese wall-hanging with which my husband had returned from his world tour in 1904 at last found a place in which it could be seen.

The smallest of these rooms, which has become known as 'Rothschild Corner' contains intimate relics connected with the family as well as early photographs of those who visited the house throughout the years. My wedding dress, made in 1913 by the famous Callot *Soeurs* can be seen here: today I can hardly believe how I ever got into it. Among other mementoes of the

Overleaf Lace from Baroness Edmond's collection. Two borders of seventeenth century Venetian needle-lace and a detail of a large stole, Brussels bobbin-lace about 1860

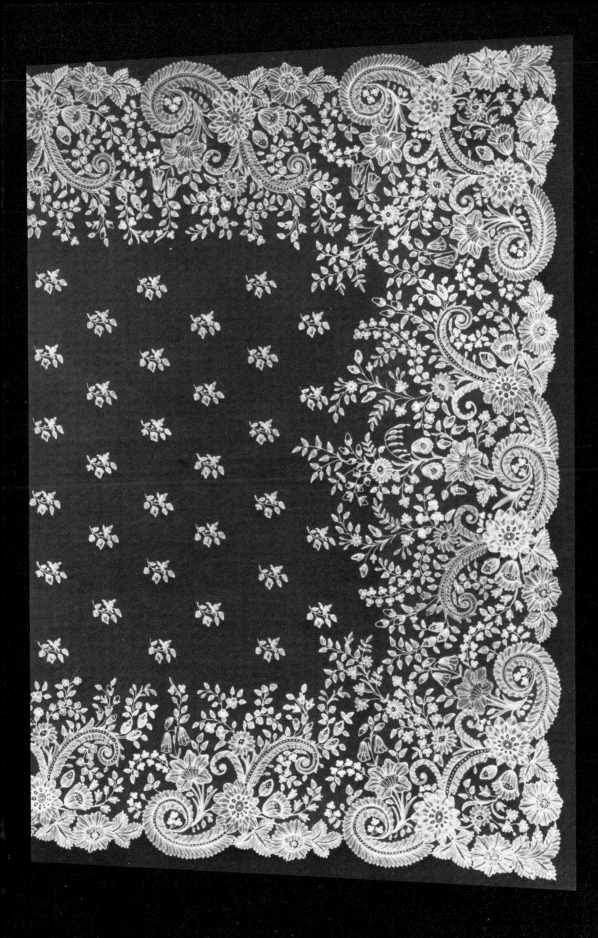

Buttons depicting winter
scenes from the collection of
Baroness Edmond

family are the results of one of my father-in-law's archaeological 'digs' in Palestine in the 1890's and commemorative scrolls in Hebrew given to Baron Ferdinand and to his successors: these frequently tax the translating powers of our guides.

Four other ex-bedrooms have completely changed their appearance. One which used to be a round chintz room in a tower has become an exotic tent containing show cases in which is displayed a complete turquoise Sèvres dessert service which in former days we cheerfuly used on grand occasions, confident that it would survive our use and the washing-up by Mrs. Green and her companions. Another bedroom contains examples of Sèvres china of the many different colours the house contained. Yet another is now called the Music Room because, to our surprise, we found there were enough old musical instruments scattered round the house to fill one room. At the other end of the house Miss Alice's collection of arms still remains on the first floor of the Bachelors' Wing, but the Billiard Room has lost its table to the one-time Still Room where it is still used and is popular among the snooker-playing residents of the house. The Billiard Room now houses some of the mediaeval illuminated manuscripts collected by Baron Edmond as well as the Savonnerie carpet which had adorned Miss Alice's private sitting room.

All this conversion of the first floor does occasionally bemuse some of our visitors who have been heard to express surprise that a house of this size should apparently have had only two bedrooms.

There also had to be some reconstruction out of doors. Waddesdon had always been most carefully maintained, particularly by Miss Alice, and we had done our best to follow her example. But I must confess there was one big exception to our endeavours and that was the aviary. Enchanting though this building is, it never figured prominently on the repainting list and during the war and the following years, it lost all priority. The result was that in 1957 it was in deplorable condition. The National Trust felt strongly that the aviary should be preserved and insisted on its repair as soon as this was feasible. No short cut towards this end was possible. The aviary's elaborate trellis work and curlicues are all made of cast iron and workmen with the necessary skill to replace the many gaps where the iron had perished through rust were not easy to find. But they were discovered eventually, and it was even perhaps fortunate that it took seven years to complete the repairs, so that the cost of putting the aviary back in order again could be spread over a number of years.

Sometimes the old days at the Manor have overlapped with

The Music Room. The
portraits of Dr Clerke
Wilshaw and his wife,
Rebecca, on either side of
the fireplace, are by Thomas
Hudson. The picture on the
right, the Daughters of Lady
Boynton, is ascribed to
Richard Cosway.

the new, and we have had visitors, grown men, often with
wives and families, who are anxious to find and point out to
their relatives the rooms in which they slept during the 1939–
45 war. It is sometimes hard to reconcile their memories with
what is now visible, but invariably they remember the big
circular staircases down which, in their infancy, and in droves,
they were urged to crawl backwards, on all fours, as the safest
means of making the descent.

Some years after their retiremnt Mrs. Green and Mabel
came to stay with me and we made what became an annual
visit of state through the house at Waddesdon. Mrs. Green's
eye-sight by now was most indifferent, but she still had a

wonderfully erect carriage and, beautifully dressed, she advanced like a ship in full sail through all the rooms at the Manor. The 'sitting wardens' were each in their place. In their youth and before marriage, many of them had worked in the house under Mrs. Green's care, but many others had not, and were what she would regard as newcomers to the village. To those in the latter category Mrs. Green's progress must have been rather startling. Moving with ceremonial tread, she halted as she came level with each 'sitting warden', bowed over to peer narrowly in her face, then seeing someone she did not recognise, clearly pronounced the single word 'No', and then moved on again. When however, she found on investigation a face that was familiar to her she enquired with impeccable memory 'Well, Violet, how are you?' or 'Now Annie, how have you been getting on?' and generally received in reply an exact account of the children and grandchildren who had been born since they had last seen Mrs. Green. Other visitors, overhearing these conversations, appeared to be puzzled that these mostly grey-haired guardians ended every sentence they addressed to Mrs. Green with the word 'Ma'am'. Times had indeed changed.

The decision to publish a comprehensive Catalogue of the contents of Waddesdon was one of the first to be taken by the National Trust when it became the new owner. I can say with my hand on my heart that we took up this task with enthusiasm. Looking back over the last twenty years I can see that at the time I had not the slightest realisation of the problems that lay ahead. We proceeded with energy and the first steps were easy, thanks to the guidance of Sir Anthony Blunt, who until recently combined the arduous duties of being Surveyor of the Queen's pictures and the Director of the Courtauld Institute. Putting his great knowledge at our disposal, he agreed to become the General Editor of the series, and found the eminent experts, both British and foreign, to write the text of each volume. The photography of all the objects to be catalogued was another winter job which took an inordinate amount of time: for many winters Mr. Eost and Mr. Macdonald, the expert photographers of the Victoria and Albert Museum can have had few Sundays free from the claims of Waddesdon. My ideas on the complexities of producing colour illustrations, as on all other preliminaries to publication, were of the haziest, but I clung to the idea that whatever malign fate might conceivably overtake Waddesdon, a published account of its contents would remain and would preserve for all time a record of the taste and knowledge of some remarkable collectors who had all been members of one family.

The Aviary, restored
between 1958 and 1965

I now have a much better comprehension of the many
detailed problems which pursue those who aim at perfection
in the technicalities of publication and my admiration for those
who solve them is unbounded. Like them, I have learnt
patience. If the leading expert in any particular field of artistic
knowledge is engaged to write a book, he will inevitably have
many other commitments which may well claim priority. And
tragedy has struck our hoped-for schedule; two of our authors
have died before their work was completed. But thanks to Sir
Anthony's persuasive powers and remarkable capacity for
work, both in discussing every detail with our authors and in
translating various foreign texts into English, the volumes continue to appear.

Happily, Waddesdon was large enough when the flats for
its present residents were constructed to include two additional
ones for visitors. Throughout the years these have been used by
the various authors of the catalogue who come to stay, when
their time permits, and study the objects of their work, some-

162

times for days on end. They are aided by Miss Rosamund Griffin who, as the Keeper at Waddesdon, not only instructs the guides on whom the public depend for information, but has the care of the condition of all the works of art. Joining the staff in the earliest days of the National Trust era she now has the greatest and most intimate knowledge of the date and history of every object in the house. The cataloguers' debt to her knowledge, and to her prowess as a calm and charming amanuensis and proof-reader, is rightly acknowledged in the foreword to every volume of the catalogue which has so far been published.

I believe Waddesdon is now inhabited by many who have as great a feeling of affection for it as any of its previous private owners. Those who live there now have to combine a capability in many professions, and be at the same time administrators, art historians and conservationists, as well as public relation experts and shopkeepers. I feel sure that Miss Alice would approve the standard of care which is still exercised and that Baron Ferdinand, that most gregarious man, would be pleased with the great number of our visitors. I hope, too, that they would both have been in favour of my attempt to follow

Baron Ferdinand feeding one
of his birds

163

their hospitable example by giving a party to celebrate the hundredth anniversary of Baron Ferdinand's purchase of the estate in September 1874. Exactly one hundred years later Waddesdon was thronged by the visiting public until late in the afternoon, so the party could not be held there; instead, it took place in a huge marquee on the lawn of the Pavilion at Eythrope. At this dinner, followed by the traditional fireworks, some four hundred people were united: members of the family; all those who worked on the estate and those who worked for the National Trust; and many others who had contributed in a wide variety of capacities to the life, embellishment or maintenance of Waddesdon throughout the years. In proposing the continued well-being of the estate, the tenant farmer whose family had had the longest tenure of their land said he remembered his father telling him to stick to Waddesdon as it was a good place in which to work. It was music in my ears to hear him say that he would still give the same advice, and for the same reason, to any young relative to-day.

Writing in 1897, Baron Ferdinand said: ' Art is a small factor in history, perhaps only an incident in it, yet it follows history in all its stages. So long as the Church and the Throne were the primary forces of civilisation it was the aim and the ambition of the artist to devote his genius to the adornment of Churches and Palaces, which he filled with all that was noblest and richest in art: but when the growth of democracy destroyed the spell of the old influence it set the artist adrift and carried away, scattering broadcast, the old artistic accumulation of ages. A new centre of attraction has been formed on the ruins of the old, produced by the very action of democracy. If the artist no longer gravitates towards the Prelate and the Prince, he now pays homage to the People, whom he idealises as an entity, competing for their patronage in academies and exhibitions, while the artistic productions of the past turn to the same magnet and pass into the hands of the People '.

Even Baron Ferdinand could hardly have foreseen the extraordinary growth of interest in the artistic possessions of this country which has come about since he wrote those words; but it is my great hope that he and both his successors would be pleased that Waddesdon has become one of the ' new centres of attraction ' of which he wrote. The very evident pleasure of our visitors seems to confirm his judgment: pleasure gives pleasure and to me it is an exceptional privilege and delight to witness it at Waddesdon year after year.

Appendices

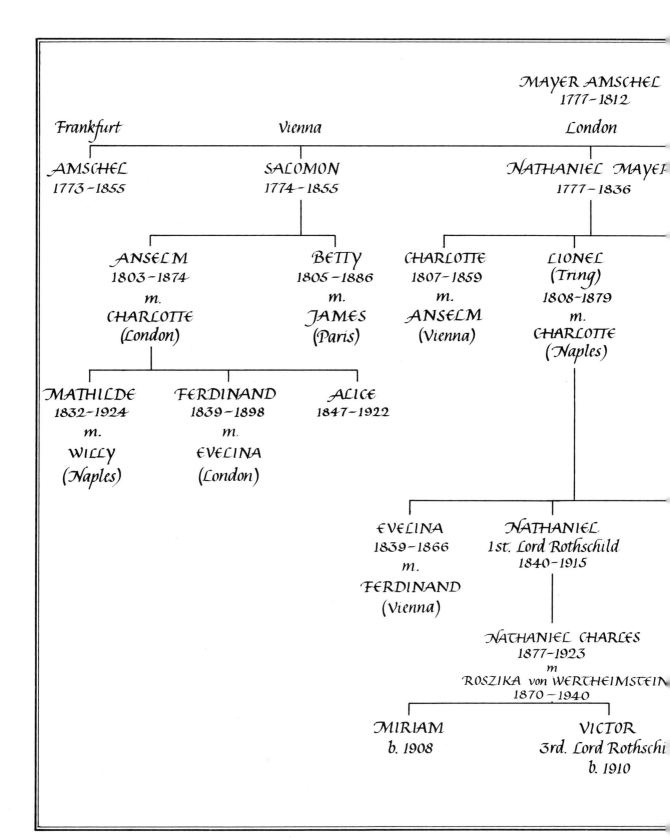

MAYER AMSCHEL
1777–1812

Frankfurt   Vienna   London

AMSCHEL
1773–1855

SALOMON
1774–1855

NATHANIEL MAYER
1777–1836

ANSELM
1803–1874
m.
CHARLOTTE
(London)

BETTY
1805–1886
m.
JAMES
(Paris)

CHARLOTTE
1807–1859
m.
ANSELM
(Vienna)

LIONEL
(Tring)
1808–1879
m.
CHARLOTTE
(Naples)

MATHILDE
1832–1924
m.
WILLY
(Naples)

FERDINAND
1839–1898
m.
EVELINA
(London)

ALICE
1847–1922

EVELINA
1839–1866
m.
FERDINAND
(Vienna)

NATHANIEL
1st. Lord Rothschild
1840–1915

NATHANIEL CHARLES
1877–1923
m
ROSZIKA von WERTHEIMSTEIN
1870–1940

MIRIAM
b. 1908

VICTOR
3rd. Lord Rothschild
b. 1910

166

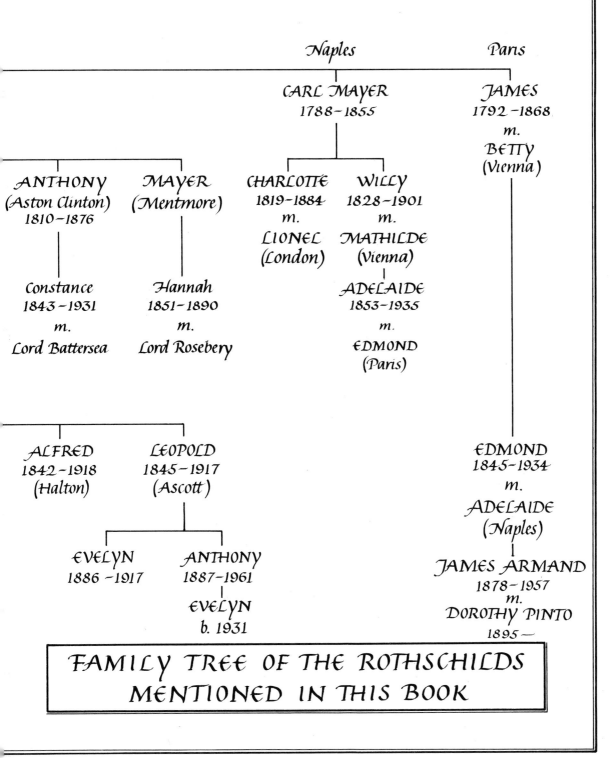

Naples   Paris

CARL MAYER
1788–1855

JAMES
1792–1868
m.
BETTY
(Vienna)

ANTHONY
(Aston Clinton)
1810–1876

MAYER
(Mentmore)

CHARLOTTE
1819–1884
m.
LIONEL
(London)

WILLY
1828–1901
m.
MATHILDE
(Vienna)

ADELAIDE
1853–1935
m.
EDMOND
(Paris)

Constance
1843–1931
m.
Lord Battersea

Hannah
1851–1890
m.
Lord Rosebery

ALFRED
1842–1918
(Halton)

LEOPOLD
1845–1917
(Ascott)

EDMOND
1845–1934
m.
ADELAIDE
(Naples)

EVELYN
1886–1917

ANTHONY
1887–1961

JAMES ARMAND
1878–1957
m.
DOROTHY PINTO
1895–

EVELYN
b. 1931

FAMILY TREE OF THE ROTHSCHILDS MENTIONED IN THIS BOOK

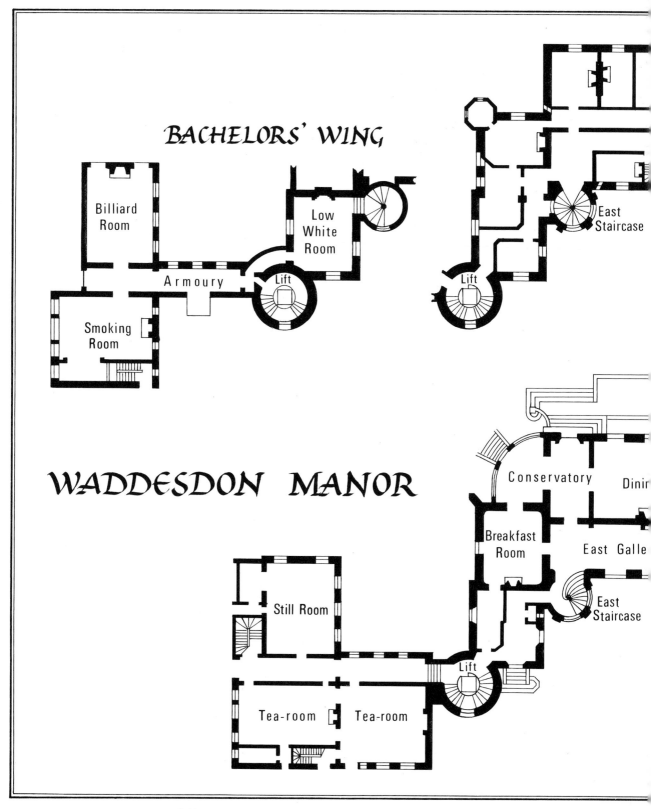

BACHELORS' WING

Billiard Room

Low White Room

Armoury

Lift

Smoking Room

East Staircase

Lift

WADDESDON MANOR

Conservatory

Dinin

Breakfast Room

East Galle

East Staircase

Still Room

Lift

Tea-room

Tea-room

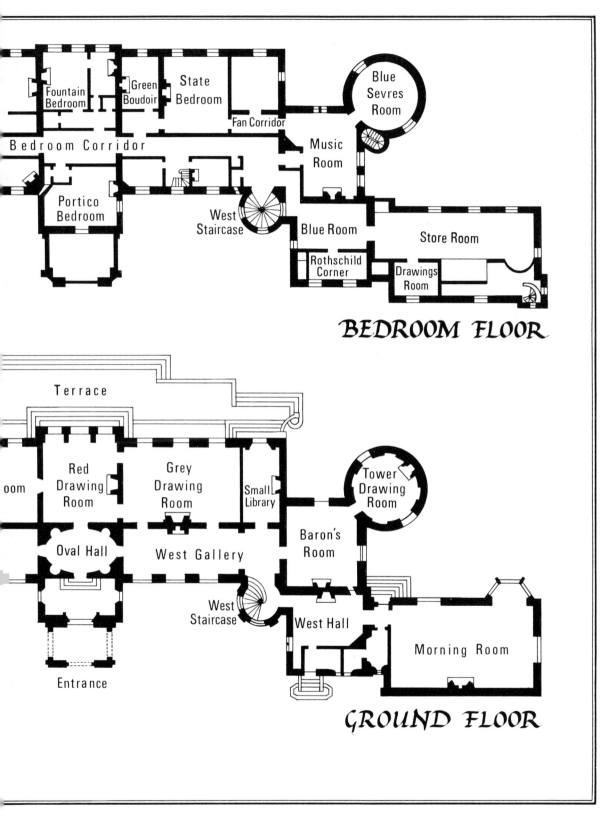

Fountain Bedroom

Green Boudoir

State Bedroom

Fan Corridor

Blue Sevres Room

Bedroom Corridor

Music Room

Portico Bedroom

West Staircase

Blue Room

Store Room

Rothschild Corner

Drawings Room

BEDROOM FLOOR

Terrace

Red Drawing Room

Grey Drawing Room

Small Library

Tower Drawing Room

oom

Oval Hall

West Gallery

Baron's Room

West Staircase

West Hall

Morning Room

Entrance

GROUND FLOOR

169

Index

171